T0198731

YOU'RE
NOT F*CKING
CRAZY

KENDRA BERGMAN

BALBOA.PRESS
A DIVISION OF HAY HOUSE

Balboa Press books may be ordered through booksellers or by contacting:

Balboa Press
A Division of Hay House
1663 Liberty Drive
Bloomington, IN 47403
www.balboapress.com
844-682-1282

Because of the dynamic nature of the Internet, any web addresses or links contained in this book may have changed since publication and may no longer be valid. The views expressed in this work are solely those of the author and do not necessarily reflect the views of the publisher, and the publisher hereby disclaims any responsibility for them.

The author of this book does not dispense medical advice or prescribe the use of any technique as a form of treatment for physical, emotional, or medical problems without the advice of a physician, either directly or indirectly. The intent of the author is only to offer information of a general nature to help you in your quest for emotional and spiritual well-being. In the event you use any of the information in this book for yourself, which is your constitutional right, the author and the publisher assume no responsibility for your actions.

Any people depicted in stock imagery provided by Getty Images are models, and such images are being used for illustrative purposes only. Certain stock imagery © Getty Images.

Front Cover artwork image design by POETREE HEALING
Editor: Sasha Banks

Print information available on the last page.

ISBN: 979-8-7652-4014-4 (sc)
ISBN: 979-8-7652-4016-8 (hc)
ISBN: 979-8-7652-4015-1 (e)

Library of Congress Control Number: 2023904521

Balboa Press rev. date: 05/31/2023

"A mixture of memoir, unfolding telepathy and invitation to trust yourself down to your spiritual core. Kendra is truly gifted." ✑

— Cathy Zipp, MS, LPC
Kick Butt Therapy Owner and
Author of *Mid-Life with Style*

"If you're a little "not f*cking crazy" like I am, you'll relate to so many things in this book and get goosebumps every time! Buy the book! It's an easy and enjoyable read."

— Barbie Thomas

"In this touching and inspiring read, Kendra Bergman shares her deeply personal spiritual experiences to assist the reader in shedding any fear or resistance they may have in giving credibility to their intuitions and insights. Her engaging stories are encouragement to pay attention to the signs and messages in our lives and the included exercises give gentle guidance on how to strengthen the connection with our inner knowing and "spirit team". This book is like a ray of light, a dear friend coming over for tea and sharing in the most interesting conversation that supports you, through reflection and anecdotes, in following your highest path and purpose."

— Serena Gabriel

"I thoroughly enjoyed reading this book, I think it is a love story. A fascinating, informative, thought provoking, and comforting read. I too have heard, seen, experienced things that are unexplainable. I aspire to embrace these feelings, they are real, and to think we can extend that to others. By sharing her story, I realize the personal challenges the author has faced while still caring for and about others making her this extraordinary person."

— Deni Mitchell

Contents

Author Statement

The purpose of this book is to assure people they are *not* crazy simply because they see images or hear voices in their mind. When our logical brain thinks about it, it cannot rationalize what is happening. Our Egoic Mind[1] jumps into action, convincing us we couldn't possibly be having these experiences and *certainly* shouldn't tell people about them. Our Egoic Mind knows these things sound crazy, "whackadoo," "woo-woo," out there, or impossible.

Humanity is waking up to the reality that our Egoic Mind doesn't know what is or is not possible.

My generation was told, "Be careful what you say, or they'll put you in the funny farm" (meaning a mental institution). Back then, little was known about mental health. The general public was simply taught that they lock up the crazy people. "They" were assumed to be the courts and "crazy people" were those who acted or thought outside of societal norms. If you were crazy, it was understood that the police would come to your home, put you in a straitjacket, and haul you away to an institution where doctors would run experiments and medicate you while they attempted a cure. Obviously, that wasn't accurate, even

---

[1] Eckhart Tolle's term for the "voice that lives in our head" and pretends to be useful when it truly is not.

back then. Now, scientists and doctors have studied the brain and human behavior enough to understand that not everything people experience that isn't understood by our egoic mind is mental illness; this is exactly the reason I want you, the person reading this book, to share your experiences.

If you have legitimate mental health issues, it is crucial and much advised that you access the professional help you need. If your experiences are simply unknown but otherwise cause no harm and bring no disruption to your life, it is important to let others who may be questioning their mental health or doubting the validity of their experiences know about them. Many people have similar experiences, and many more are becoming brave enough to talk about them. Don't overthink it. Get out of your own way. Do your research. Just know you are not alone, and you are *not* crazy.

This book includes experiences shared by beautiful souls who have released their fear of judgment or being labeled as crazy. As we share our thoughts and beliefs, we often find ourselves surrounded by others who are like-minded. There are so many people who have a vast array of experiences to share, and it is vital that we accept them and continue to share love, joy, and peace with others to raise the vibrational energy throughout the world into Oneness.

Introduction:
The Two-by-Four Effect

> **Sometimes I think there are only two instructions we need to follow to develop and deepen our spiritual life: slow down and let go.**
> **—Oriah Mountain Dreamer**

As I lay in my hospital bed with the door closed, unable to sleep anymore, I decided it was a good time to quiet my mind and follow my nurse's directives to meditate. The chaos that preceded this moment warranted an intentional pause, but I was not expecting nor was I prepared for what would happen in this meditation. I saw things I could not have made up in my mind and heard things I would not have said in speaking to myself.

I closed my eyes and took a few deep breaths, listening to the rhythm of my breath and focusing all my attention on it. As I concentrated, my mind asked, *What is the lesson here?* I heard the words "slow down" so loudly and with such densely booming clarity that I opened my eyes to see who had sneaked into my room. Nobody was there. I stared at the wall across the room. I heard it again, slowly and distinctly, this time with several voices in unison:

"Slowwww down!"

My mind responded silently, *I can't.* I closed my eyes again and a surprising dialogue began. "You can. You did. But it took hitting you over the head with a two-by-four," the voices said, matter-of-factly. "This is what you get when you ignore us." I felt tears streaming down my face but kept my eyes closed and remained focused on the conversation.

I've been busy. I had to take care of mom and get that contract proposal out. It's my whole life.

"No. It is not your whole life—that is what we have been telling you. Slow down." The conversation continued as though I was talking to a group of friends on a conference call. I couldn't see them. I didn't know who they all were, but I somehow *knew* they were several beings from my spirit team. I had no doubt they had been trying to get my attention. The truth was that I had been ignoring them for two months. I made the choice to straight up shut them out, even ignoring the ringing in my ears (a clear sign that the other side was communicating)—a choice that would prove costly.

Stubborn and Thick-Headed

I saw this title to a podcast recently: *The Lengths Your Angels Will Go To.* I laughed out loud and said, "Yup! They will hit you over the head with a two-by-four." Throughout my life, I have been called stubborn and thick-headed. My dad said it best even when I was a child. He would frequently ask me, "Do we have to hit you over the head with a two-by-four just to get your attention?" He did not mean it literally, of course. It's like some of the scenes in the *Back to the Future* movie series. One of the characters is consistently smacked on the head as someone sarcastically yells, "Hello, McFly!" Listening to others is, admittedly, not one of my greatest strengths.

Sometimes I still must be (figuratively) smacked over the head to get the message someone is telling me. People will tell me the same thing more than once, or in multiple ways for me to understand. My friends and family accept it as a personality trait. When someone tells me the same thing they told me yesterday, they are not being redundant; they are making sure I got the message. The Universe also knows this about me and does not judge. I have come to realize I usually receive signals, symbols, or messages in a series of three when it is important. Sometimes, though, I am closed off. I am busy with other things and don't notice the signs. Or, when I do notice them, I ignore them because they don't seem like a priority in the moment.

Although there is a clear path for our life here, we also have free will. Using our free will, we make choices that guide our life. Perhaps we step off the main path, making a random choice the Universe didn't expect. It may divert us for a while. Kind of like taking a side trail off the main hiking path. We may even get lost along that trail and wander a bit. At some point, though, we encounter rocks or find another trail that leads us back to the main path.

The Universe has much to teach us about how to live a healthy and prosperous life on earth, but we must not resist where it guides us.

When I resist the guidance, ignore the messages, and prioritize other things, the Universe will get my attention. It is basically the same as hitting me over the head with a two-by-four. It is usually unpleasant, often dramatic. It usually stops everything I am doing in my day-to-day life until I learn the lesson or get the message. Sometimes it happens very fast and without any warning. There have been several of these events during my lifetime. I now simply refer to them as "the two-by-four effect."

> **To see a World in a grain of sand, and a Heaven in a wild flower, hold Infinity in the palm of your hand, and Eternity in an hour.**
> **—William Blake**

The First Real Two-by-Four

When I was a young adult, I left my hometown with my infant son and moved across the country. I went to live with my in-laws in North Carolina. My husband at the time was away in the military. His parents had a young daughter they wanted me to nanny. It would be a new town in a new part of the country. The move seemed like a grand adventure! I had never lived far away from my parents or friends. My parents tried to warn me. They suggested rather than a move, maybe a trip would be better. They tried to reason with me. I had never even met my in-laws! My sister tried to convince me to stay. My friends supported the trip but were wary of a move so far from home.

I ignored them all.

I convinced myself it would be just like a long vacation. More importantly, I was determined to make it on my own. So, I had all our belongings packed and sent to North Carolina.

Bright eyed and full of curiosity, I got on a plane with my three-month-old baby boy and headed east. I was determined to prove to my family, friends, and mostly to myself that I was moving forward in my life. I could make it in the big world without depending on them.

The adventure started off in a bumpy way, as many new things do. Any concerns I had came and went. I ignored the red flags. It was summertime. The beach was a five-minute walk away. My five-year-old sister-in-law, my infant son, and I were all able to spend most days there, which kept the extreme discomfort I felt at bay ... or so I thought. I found myself rationalizing day after day the decision to move and the benefits of being there. I was homesick. I was away from home, emotional, and potentially experiencing some postpartum depression. The uneasy feeling of being in a new place was part of the natural process of a move. However, I soon became aware that my in-law's lifestyle did not fit with my values and morals, and it was not the way I wanted my son to be raised.

I was a bit naive, having lived a fairly sheltered life. It took me a few weeks to realize they were dealing drugs. From there it was like a lightbulb came on when I recognized they were also *using* drugs. They did not keep them safely hidden or away from their little girl. I could not understand or accept their way of life. Within a month of relocating to the east coast, I began wondering how I could move back home.

Hurricane season began a few weeks later with a storm heading directly toward us. I was not prepared for any of the things I was experiencing. The night that the storm made landfall, I knew I could not stay. As I tried to soothe my baby to sleep, I promised him it would be OK. I cried and told him I would keep him safe. I told him we would find a way out. Financially, it seemed impossible. I resigned myself to accepting the circumstances for a while because the last thing I wanted to do was ask my family for help. I did not want to admit that they had been right. I did not want to accept that they'd given me good advice. It would take time to save the money for airfare, but I could make it work in a few months.

I soon started making phone calls to my parents and family. Without telling them the circumstances, I let them know that the place was not for me. I did not admit that I was wrong, or that they knew better, only that it was temporary and was always intended to be temporary. I told them that I was just planning to shorten the stay there by a few months. Every week or two, I shipped a box back home without my in-laws knowing. I did not want to seem ungrateful or create conflict between us.

You have to be a responsible adult, I kept telling myself. I was too proud to ask for financial help from my parents and was determined to do it on my own. I would be the one to get us out of this mess.

There was no sense of urgency because I was not in an unsafe environment. There was no abuse or physical danger to us. Occasionally people would come to the house to make (somewhat) discrete deals. My son and I would conveniently go to the beach or take a nap in my room. I was determined to stick it out, even though every fiber in my being told me I should get back home to the people I trusted. My parents knew how stubborn I could be. They gently offered some help, knowing that if I really needed money, I would ask for it. They allowed me to be a little too proud. I refused to fail as I had done so many times before. Stubborn and thick-headed as usual.

It was less than three months later when the two-by-four came. My spirit team and I had been out of touch for years. They were probably screaming, "Get out." I simply would not hear them, but the Universe knew better and used that old trusty two-by-four to get my attention. My dad was in the hospital. He was a man who was stronger than anyone I had ever known. He never went to the doctor. He was always healthy and vibrant, and even more stubborn. He never got sick other than an occasional migraine, which he cured with a hot shower and sleep. He never complained and apparently had an incredible tolerance for pain.

The night my mom called to tell me he was hospitalized, she was as surprised as anyone. Her day had started like any other until he asked her to take him to the doctor (our family doctor of twenty years). He was doubled over in excruciating abdominal pain. She wanted to take him to the hospital, but he insisted on seeing the family doctor instead. As soon as they walked into the office, the doctor took one look at his face and told my mom to immediately take him to the hospital. Once he was admitted, the medical team began their tests. My father had gallstones—and not just stones—his gallbladder was so full and inflamed that it was double the size of a normal one. Needless to say, they scheduled him for emergency surgery.

When the call came that his health was in jeopardy, all my pride completely evaporated. I had always put my dad on a pedestal. He was my superhero. I asked my mom to buy me a plane ticket. There was absolutely no doubt I was going home now, for good. Fortunately for me, my in-laws were out of town, which meant there would be no one there to ask any questions.

I don't remember packing or how I even got home. The only thing I remember is walking into the hospital room and seeing a shell of a man. The surgery was successful, but he experienced several challenging weeks before finally recovering.

That time, the two-by-four had hit me over the head to make me get out of my own way and allow others to help me. It forced me to accept the fact that I cannot always do things on my own. I needed to understand that moving away from my family was not an escape or the way to prove myself as an adult.

Knocking on Death's Door

One thing you commonly hear from those who have had NDEs (near death experiences) is, "It all happened so fast." My experience was no exception. It was lunchtime and I had just hung up from a phone call with my niece. I stood at the kitchen counter to quickly reheat some leftovers while having an intense conversation with my husband, Paul. My father had passed away two months prior. I was telling Paul of the written plans our niece requested that would ensure our final wishes were known and carried out. After our conversation, he went into his home office for a conference call. I also had work to do from home. My back was aching from a previous two-by-four session with the Universe, so I headed to the bed to work on my laptop while laying down.

Less than an hour later I went into septic shock.

I could feel in my body that something wasn't right. I needed to use the restroom, urgently. As I sat on the toilet, things began to escalate. I suddenly had to grab the trash can as I began to vomit uncontrollably. Everything was happening at once.

It seemed as though all the fluids in my body were in a hurry to escape my body. I grew hotter and hotter. I was sweating. When I thought it was over, I crawled onto the floor to lay myself down on the cool bathroom tile in front of the sink. I was only there for a few minutes when another bout began, and I was back on the toilet with the trash can on my lap.

Once again, I thought it was over. I was certain there could not be any fluids left. I melted onto the floor to place my face on the cool tile again. I was too weak to get a cool washcloth. I considered yelling for Paul, but before I could, it was like I was watching a TV show with me in it. I could see what Paul would find if he walked around the corner into the bathroom. I was scared for him to see me on the floor sprawled out and barely able to move. At that moment, I knew I was dying.

Suddenly, I felt something literally pull me back up onto the toilet— something I could not have done myself as I was growing weaker by the second. I'd had the presence of mind to bring my cell phone into the bathroom with me and vaguely remember texting Paul, "I need ambulance." I went back down onto the tile and soon after, Paul arrived in the calm and collected manner one would expect from a retired police officer. The first words I heard him say were filled with concern. "Honey, honey, honey! Can I drive you to the emergency room?" "I won't make it," I replied, barely able to speak. Paul immediately phoned 911, maintaining his calm professionalism with the operator so well that the ambulance showed up without turning on its lights or sirens.

A gurney had been wheeled into our bathroom. However, by this time I was back on the toilet, which is in a tiny room separated from the sinks and shower. One of the paramedics asked me if I thought I'd be able to get myself onto the gurney, which was about eight feet away. I could only shake my head no as the vomiting continued. He said he'd give me a minute and to let them know when I was ready. I heard one of them asking Paul all the questions. What medications did I take? What had I eaten? How long had this been going on?

After gathering what waning strength I had, I essentially flung myself from the toilet seat and fell onto the gurney. They put me in the ambulance. Paul was there with them, telling me he would meet me at the hospital. I was fading. I could no longer speak and couldn't keep my eyes open. I could hear one of the paramedic's concerns when she was unable to get a blood pressure reading. As another paramedic took over, I must have passed out. The next thing I remembered was my gurney being pulled from the ambulance. There was definitely a sense of urgency. I heard them quickly rattle off my vitals to the hospital staff. "BP seventy over forty. Temp 96°. Pulse …" I faded out of consciousness again.

It seemed time had stopped. When I woke up, hours had passed. Paul and my mom were in the private emergency room with me. Doctors searched for an explanation and answers as to the cause. Was it bad food? No, my husband had literally eaten and drank the exact same thing I had the previous night. Was it medication or drugs? No, everything I took was the night before as usual and prescribed by a doctor. Was it an unknown disease? Scans, blood tests, urine tests, stool tests. The hospital had acted quickly and brought me back from the brink of death, but I was still very sick. They were baffled. I wanted to yell, "Call Dr. House!" But even in my delusional state, I knew he was fictional. By the time they transferred me to the ICU, I had a sense of certainty that I would be OK; so much so, that I kept Paul from notifying my sons or our nieces and nephews of the situation. I was going to make it. Even my mom had gone home by that point.

The cause never became clear, but I gradually improved while more doctors and specialists than I could count continued to run tests and administer multiple medications. As the days passed, I was downgraded from the ICU and transferred level by level into other units in the hospital.

When I was finally ready to be discharged from the hospital, the gastrointestinal specialist chalked it up to a "best guess" explanation, but by then I knew the technical cause was meaningless. It was a two-by-four to get my attention. I had been ignoring the Universe for what I thought were more important things at the time. Now, there was no doubt. No forgetting, minimizing, or moving on. My health was the most important priority, and without it, none of the other things I prioritized would even be possible. I got the message loud and clear.

The health crisis was the two-by-four, but the messages still needed to be heard, understood, and processed. I soon became restless and impatient. The doctors concluded the main factor in my health decline was due to the immense stress I had allowed to consume my life. I knew I had to make drastic changes but wasn't sure what pieces of my life I could rearrange or let go. I asked my husband, hospital staff, and the Universe, "How?!"

As my nurse, Gabby, cared for me and prepared me for self-care at home, she strongly recommended meditation. Right. I knew that. *I am a yoga instructor,* I thought. I was even taking an advanced course studying the depths of meditation. Why wasn't I practicing what I preached? I had been good at my mediation practice until the train went off the tracks two months earlier.

Gabby didn't just tell me to meditate once and let it go. She repeated it on three separate occasions each day that I was a patient under her care. She had a second job working with veterans with post-traumatic stress disorder and had seen the benefits. She used meditation as an important tool to manage her own stress. After the third time, I knew it was an important sign or message. I thought about it, seeking the "right" opportunity, and finally took the advice.

I had been blessed with a private room for the entire hospital stay. Other than my husband, visitors had not been allowed for the first several days due to the potential high contagion. Even as my health stabilized, there were too many questions about the cause, so I strongly discouraged anyone else from visiting. The television was of little interest to me. I began listening to guided meditations to pass the time. Finally, I convinced myself to really meditate. The conditions were optimal, and I knew I had to meditate with a completely open mind and heart.

Compared with other experiences I had had in meditations, this one was unbelievable. Yes—unbelievable. Isn't that the term we use for something that doesn't make sense? Something that sounds crazy? Something that, if we told other people, they would not believe? They would think we were crazy. But it happened. The experience was real and clear; it profoundly changed my life.

The Universe is our greatest teacher, even in its harshest lessons.

Mindfulness Exercise | *Creating Your Space*

Consciously carve out time for yourself in a quiet environment. Create a feeling of peace (saying a prayer, lighting candles or incense, turning on some soothing music). Get into a comfortable position and direct your attention to your breath as you gently close your eyes. Repeat these words silently or out loud. *I deserve this time to relax and care for myself.* When you are ready, open your eyes and write whatever comes to mind on the lines below.

_____

_____

_____

_____

_____

_____

_____

_____

_____

_____

Wendee Grinde, age 54

Goodbye my friends, I must be gone, from this world, to a life beyond. But remember I am with you still, in the rainbow and the daffodil. In a flower, in a butterfly, you can hear my spirit sigh. And then someday, I don't know when, we will all be together again.

—Melody J. Carolan

My mother wrote this poem during the two years she lived with cancer. I read this poem the day we laid her ashes into the ground. As you can imagine, butterflies mean a great deal to me. I would see a butterfly lingering around and a smile would appear on my face as I thought of a lost loved one. But the story I am going to share describes how that simple creature that brings joy to my heart, delivered a message from my father.

I lost my father suddenly in June 2019 after a dangerous fall. He was starting to show little signs of dementia prior to his accident, so we had several discussions about how he'd like things to be carried out once he was gone. One of his wishes was that I show love and care to his wife. I consider myself a forgiving person who tries to rise above the drama, but I struggled one day, upon learning that his wife hated me and blamed me for my father's death. I tried so earnestly to make her and her (adult) children comfortable that I began to neglect my own feelings.

All manner of emotions were stirring up inside of me. I was alone, at home, cleaning, and crying when I saw something. I looked up to see a large, dark butterfly fluttering around my dining room light. It was at that moment, when I felt peace. I felt that my father was telling me that everything was going to be OK.

So why did *this* butterfly deliver me more than just a joyful feeling? Perhaps it was because of the emotional state I was in at the moment. Perhaps I wanted to feel my father's presence, or it might've been because I was simply in awe that there was a butterfly actually fluttering around inside my home. Whatever anyone else might think, I know that his presence was with me, calming me down and allowing me to feel his love. He (the butterfly) stayed with me until I fell asleep and was gone when I woke up the next morning.

Vibrations and Frequencies

The real voyage of discovery consists not in seeking new landscapes, but in having new eyes.

—Marcel Proust

Everything has a vibration—every single thing. These days, there is more information about vibrations than ever before. Vibrations create energy. You may have heard of chakras, which are subtle energy centers ("subtle" because they cannot be seen by most people) within all humans. Chakras have been taught for thousands of years. The word chakra is an ancient Sanskrit word that translates to *wheel*. These wheels are spinning with an energetic flow, and they affect all aspects of your life, whether you realize it or not. There are seven main wheels spinning within our beings. I encourage you to read a book or take a course on chakras to learn more about subtle energies. These energy centers control how the energy flows for every aspect of your life.

There is scientific proof, which can be seen and felt, of vibrations turning into energy. All these different vibrations are on a frequency, like a satellite or the internet. If you spend time thinking about it from a place of true open-mindedness, the awareness of vibrations and frequencies makes complete sense. You don't have to see the vibration for it to be there. Much the way that Bluetooth devices connect through an unseen field of energy, you don't have to touch a dial or push a button to tune into a high-vibrational frequency.

Electricity vibrates to create an energetic field. We know one can get shocked when touching certain wires. Lightning is energetically tuned into the electricity frequency, which can be so powerful it can kill a person. On a dry day in our house, we used to drag our feet on the carpet, walk up to someone, lightly touch them, and watch them jump from the little shock. It doesn't happen unless all the circumstances align—the vibration created must tune into the correct frequency; if you don't wear shoes, it rarely happens; if you don't touch with just the right pressure, it won't happen; if the air is humid, it usually doesn't happen. Why not? Taking a balloon and rubbing it on your dry hair tunes the electricity to a frequency we can see and feel. If you create enough static electricity, the balloon will stay on a wall and defy gravity while the vibration is just right for that frequency.

We know that sound vibrates. A thunderstorm or low-flying jet rattles the windows. Soprano opera singers' voices can break glass. It is obvious that the glass reacts to the vibration of sound. Singing bowls vibrate to create a tone that lasts as long as the bowl is vibrating. When you hold the bowl still as it is played, you can feel the vibration. The sounds of our voices are vibrations of the vocal cords. The words and sounds we make with our vocal cords create an energy. This is why positive affirmations have become so popular. Speaking those words, especially out loud through a vibration, creates an energy that connects to a higher frequency.

Mindfulness Exercise | *Vocal Vibration*

Take a deep breath in and exhale. As you take another deep breath in, prepare your mind to create a vocal vibration by simply humming. As you exhale, keep your lips together and hum. Can you feel the vibration in your throat? Place your hand gently on the front of your neck as you do it again. Can you feel it now? You are creating a vibration that is audible and inside your being. The vibration is connected to a frequency. Perhaps you are familiar with the sound of "OM" also known as "AUM." Try the same exercise making the sound *OM*.

> **OM (aka AUM) is the sound of cosmic consciousness. OM Mantra used in meditation creates a vibration that represents three states of our ordinary consciousness; waking, dream, and deep sleep.**
>
> —Gayatri Clabnova

_____

_____

_____

_____

_____

_____

Self-Talk

People joke about talking to themselves, but everyone does it. And it's not about talking to ourselves. I grew up in a family where we would talk out loud, and when asked who we were talking to, the response was always the same: "Myself." Inevitably, there would be some crack about people thinking we were crazy. There it is. Once again, society has imposed an idea upon us based on a few examples. Do genuinely insane or mentally ill people talk to themselves? Yes! However, most of us are simply socialized into not talking out loud to ourselves in public to avoid a stigma. We still talk, just not out loud. It is important to observe our thoughts (known now as *self-talk*) and question where they are coming from.

My egoic mind will sometimes run wild if I don't stay alert. I learned to recognize my egoic mind by watching my thoughts. If I observe what I am thinking, I can catch the egoic mind generating negative thoughts. When we are unaware, it can spin out of control, often sending us into depressive episodes and other difficult emotional cycles that can be very hard to wade through. When our spirit team is speaking to us, the difference is in the message. Our spirit team will never speak to us negatively or insultingly; they are here purely to love us, protect us, and guide us to a higher vibrational frequency.

Sixth Sense

So far science can only account for the use of about 10 percent of the brain. Yet through imaging, neuroactivity can be identified throughout 100 percent of the entire brain. What is the other 90 percent doing? What senses do we have that are unproven? Many have heard of the "sixth sense." Do you get a feeling of a police officer being near when you are speeding and then see one a few miles down the road? Do you have an idea of what you want for dinner and discover your partner was thinking of the exact same thing? Do you feel an urge to contact a friend or relative and find out they are going through a tough time or were about to contact you? Do you actually believe it is all coincidence? I've heard Deepak Chopra call it "synchronicity." Somewhere deep within our souls, we know there are other senses.

The voices we hear are real. I'm talking about the positive messages, reminders, or warnings we hear all throughout the day and night. (Of course, anything that guides us or tells us to harm ourselves or others in any way warrants that we seek medical attention immediately.) Let's be honest: the brain is a complex organ. The chemicals can be off just the same way sugar levels are off for diabetics or blood pressure that is too high or too low. In these circumstances, only trained medical professionals can help. The voices I'm talking about are the "internal dialogues" that often sound like our own voice, the one telling us to take the long way to the store instead of the short way. The voice that warns us that we might spill a drink. The voice that jolts us out of bed at night, alerting us to turn on the dishwasher. There are so many, and they happen so frequently that it is difficult to discern what is coming from our own egoic mind and what is coming from a higher power.

According to the Cleveland Clinic, "Your brain determines every aspect of your life and without your brain, there is no self and no awareness of the world. Your brain is a three-pound universe that processes 70,000 thoughts each day using 100 billion neurons that connect at more than 500 trillion points through synapses that travel 300 miles/hour."[2]

Pause for a moment and consider what would happen if even *just 1 percent* of those "thoughts" were actually coming from a higher source. Can you imagine your life if seven hundred of the thoughts you had in a day were guiding you in a direction that kept you safe, protected, loved, joyful, and prosperous?

---

[2] *Healthy Brains* by Cleveland Clinic

Love

Love vibrates to the highest known frequency, creating an energy that is palpable. The first time we fall in love and touch the person who is the object of our affection, we "feel" a connection. Sometimes it is literally electric. Love is a vibration. The best thing we can do for ourselves, and the world, is to consciously and intentionally raise our energetic vibration to tune into the good frequencies.

All That Is

Author, healer, podcast host, and educator Julie Jancius says, "Energy vibrates. We know that everything is energy. And all energy vibrates at different levels or different frequencies. The highest vibration that is, is God energy. God is everyone and everything. All of the different terms people use are all used to describe the same thing." Eckart Tolle refers to it as *The Now*. Star Wars fans may recognize it referred to as *The Force*. Some call it universal love energy or reiki energy healing. It's the most powerful energy there is.

Spread High Vibrations and Loving Energy

For thousands of years, our ancestors have been telling the tale. They have explained in books, ancient writings, and drawings the importance of tuning into the correct frequency with the vibrations created by our thoughts, words, and actions. You can feel a connection with a throat vibration, and it can be shared and affect others.

Vibrations can even tune multiple energies together to the same frequency, unseen and simultaneously. Monks use gongs and chanting to create a vibration of love and peace while connecting their frequencies together.

As we raise our vibration and tune into the universal love frequency, we can begin to easily sense energy. Have you ever walked into a room and instantly known what the "vibe" was? We can feel how the energy of the room is vibrating because all beings have a vibrational energy. If the energy is low, heavy, or negative, we can *feel* it. At a motivational speaking event or conference, the emcee or coordinator will raise the vibration in the room. It might be with words, using the vocal vibration tuned to a positive frequency. It might be an upbeat music vibration. It might even be a moment of silence in gratitude or love.

Some earlier generations defied the stigma of being "crazy" in an attempt to teach us the importance of positive energies versus negative energies. Jesus, Yogananda, Buddha, and Krishna are just a few of the popular ones. Even before their time on earth, people drew petroglyphs on walls. Interestingly, similar images can be found all over the world. Across centuries, different cultures around the world were all trying to convey the same message. Somehow that message became misperceived, distorted, and altered, dividing much of the world into different organized religions. Contemplate how we could all feel if humanity would all come together and vibrate at similar frequencies of joy, love, ease, peace, grace, and bliss. History tells us that it is not plausible, but every effort changes something, and we can all make small changes.

Scientific studies have proven earlier cultures were correct. Energy can be shared with another person or people. Yawning is often considered contagious. Smiling at a stranger can raise the energetic vibration within another person, causing them to smile back and lifting their mood. They might spread it by smiling at another stranger. Maintaining our own high vibrations and tuning into the frequencies of God, Angels, Guides, The Divine, All That Is, I Am, Spirit, or the Universe to spread love, gratitude, and joy is in our destiny.

Mindfulness Exercise | *Spreading Loving Kindness*

Take a few moments to bring in the image and be mindful about someone you care for deeply. Think of three things you love about them. *Feel* the love and compassion in your heart. Then take a deep breath in, and as you exhale, visualize that loving kindness and compassion spreading out to fill up your home, your street, your city, touching neighbors, friends, and even strangers. Continue to expand that loving energy wider and wider until you have shared it with your whole state, country, and the entire world. Take another breath in as you smile, knowing you have raised the vibration of others, even if you cannot see it. You have spread loving kindness to others. Use the space below to write any thoughts or feelings after this exercise.

_____

_____

_____

_____

_____

_____

_____

_____

_____

Listen to the Children

When babies look beyond you and giggle, maybe they're seeing angels.
—Eileen Elias Freeman

We begin asking questions at a young age. First by learning and speaking silently with our mind. As we learn speech, we ask those around us who are responsible for all decisions. "Can I wear the green shirt?" "Can I have fish sticks?" "Can I stay up past my bedtime?" Many children have what we call "imaginary friends." What if the child is seeing something or is aware of something that the adults are unaware of? The adults accuse them of lying, make fun of them, or at the very least, call it imaginary.

If you listen to children—really listen—they are very wise. They are so tuned into the communication frequency that they learn a language. Some children are taught multiple languages at a young age. I have a friend whose granddaughter learned English, Hungarian, and sign language before she was three. She had a full vocabulary in all three languages! Let's consider any telepathic or intuitive language she may also know if she tuned into those frequencies. Some people compare children to sponges, soaking up all the knowledge and information around them.

What if children are older souls here to teach us lessons? What if they have abilities we disregard, ignore, or suppress as we domesticate them? What if imaginary friends are simply spirits from the other side? What would people be like if we encouraged them as my parents did with me?

When my nephew was about three years old, he boldly announced one day, "I'm from another planet!" We all laughed and assumed he was trying to get attention. My sister asked, "What planet?" He thought for a moment and then answered, "Weirdo planet." Again, we laughed and went on with whatever we were doing before his big announcement. We didn't tell him he was wrong. We didn't tell him it was impossible. We also didn't encourage him or ask more questions. A few months later he brought it up again. "Grandma, I'm from Weirdo Planet," he said. It became a joke. "Well, that explains a lot!" We never forgot it. As time passed, we would joke with him, domesticating him into realizing we were making fun of what he had said years ago. He stopped talking about it and rolled his eyes whenever we brought it up. Out of the mouth of an innocent child comes the most amazing things.

We must open our minds and truly listen and ask ourselves, *Is it really just imagination?* The word "imagination" is defined as "something not actually present to the senses." Now, consider if the definition was "something not actually present to the *known* senses." If you are hearing voices or seeing things, it does not fit into this specific definition of imagination because each of those things is produced from your known senses. However, we refer to it as such all the time. If it's not our imagination, it seems crazy, right? No, it is not crazy.

The world is now awakening and accepting that the voices, images, feelings, or sense of knowingness we have are *real*.

As I studied religious philosophies, I learned about reincarnation. One lesson struck me as the professor explained that many children are born with memories of their past life, but as new memories of this life fill in, they forget their previous lifetime experiences. It immediately took me back to that moment of my nephew's announcement—maybe he *was* from another planet. At least another dimension or someplace we could not recognize. Because we could not understand, he referred to it as a planet, but maybe he was talking about the other side.

I am not so egotistical as to think earth is the only planet with life on it. Perhaps he is from another planet. I know that he was born into this physical life. He is here to do great things and teach many lessons. It apparently began with teaching our family not to dismiss everything children tell us as imaginary even if those things don't make sense.

People grow up in societies and cultures conditioned to ignore, dismiss, or keep these things to themselves for fear of being called crazy. We are not crazy! We are aware and open. We are awake!

> **Train up a child in the way he should go: and when he is old, he will not depart from it. (Proverbs 22:16 KJV)**

Parents' Encouragement

My parents always read books and stories about unconventional subjects. They believed in the Bible, and they also knew of abilities and energy that were not mainstream knowledge in our American culture. They were not crazy—they were educated and knowledgeable about unconventional concepts and theories.

Some were controversial subjects such as what we now know as NDE (near death experiences) and ESP (extrasensory perception). My parents spent time with my sister and me, encouraging and teaching us, just as if we were learning another language. They taught us we could discover and learn things other than what was taught in school. A couple of powerful memories stand out.

When I was about six years old, my mom decided to try an exercise with me to see if what she was reading about ESP could be true. As an adult, I now realize she was also probably trying to entertain me and pass the time because dinner was later than usual. My dad occasionally worked late into the evenings in real estate. I remember the event because of the feeling of pride and accomplishment for having special abilities. My mom probably has many more details and a more accurate account.

My mom had me lie down on the couch, close my eyes, and relax my mind. She probably walked me through what we now refer to as a guided meditation. She told me to imagine my dad at work. Even though I had never been to his office, she encouraged me to *imagine* it, to pretend I was there watching him. She asked me about everything I saw in my imagination, encouraging me to look closer and describe in detail some items I mentioned. At one point, I saw a picture on his wall next to his desk. I vaguely remember seeing mountains, but not like mountains in a painting or out our window. There were lines and bumps on the picture. A few minutes later, my dad called. I assumed he called to tell her he was coming home soon so she could prepare dinner. As I lay there on the couch, she asked my dad questions about what I had described. They were both amazed when my dad confirmed a topographic map hung on the wall next to his desk! I had no idea what they were referring to, but the comparison of descriptions made sense to all three of us. ESP was real, and I had it.

Whether my memory is accurate or not matters little.

The memory of encouragement from my parents allowed my mind to be open. It created a safe environment for me to talk to them about anything "strange" or different. I knew they would listen without judgment and not dismiss what I said simply because I was a child. Of course, they did have to really listen and evaluate, as I still told untruths and tested their boundaries. I was by no means an easy child to raise. It takes a special skill set to be parents who both encourage children while teaching them respect and the value of truth. As I look back now, I can see where they must have listened to their own spirit teams to discern what I was experiencing and imagining versus untruths. They never seriously believed I was crazy, but there were definitely societal beliefs put in my head to ensure I did not take advantage of their open minds.

The Bible says, "With God, all things are possible." It is true, especially if we allow and encourage our children to explore all possibilities.

LaDonna Bergman, age 81

We were raised to know God, and my parents and grandparents told stories of the Bible. Most nights after dinner, the whole family would gather at the piano and sing hymns or popular songs. After we moved to Tucson, Mother taught Sunday School, Daddy sang in choir, and us "children" were in youth groups or junior choir. Our faith was very strong then.

After four of us were married and some had children, we all visited our parents close to once a week. When my mother was in her early sixties, she went to the hospital with horrible pain in her side. They did all kinds of tests and found that a gallstone had passed into a duct, and she had pancreatitis. She was on IVs and pills, but they let my dad spend time with her. One afternoon she almost died. The IV had run dry, and she passed out until nurses came in and found it. I think she said it was five or ten minutes. They let four of the five of us in to see her. Afterward, we discussed whether to call our sister in San Diego to come, but after praying to God, I told them I thought Mother would be fine.

Several years later, my mother told me what she had never forgotten about that day. She said she felt like she was going up in the air like in a tube, hearing joyful singing and seeing gorgeous flowers and beautiful colors on the way. Then a voice asked if she wanted to continue or to stay on Earth. She was sure it was God. She said she wanted to see all her grandchildren get married before she left Earth. And *whoosh*—she returned to the hospital and the pain.

She recovered from that episode and enjoyed her family and husband for many years after, although she had more health issues along with the arthritis she had had for years: uterine cancer with radiation, back surgery, gallbladder surgery, neuropathy, and more. But she enjoyed the family, Christmases, birthdays, and her grandchildren. She watched them all get married and enjoyed great-grandchildren! She lived to be eight-nine years old.

Have You Ever?

You'll see it when you believe it.
—Wayne Dyer

Have you ever had the same thought as your best friend, partner, or family member at the same time? You laugh, you agree you know each other well, and assume it's coincidence. What if it isn't? What if it was a guardian angel whispering in both of your ears the same thing at the same time? To take it a step deeper, what if you were communicating telepathically?

As a teenager, my family had a routine: my dad would come home from work, lie down on the couch, and take a nap while my mom made dinner. One evening, I was engrossed in the movie *Little Darlings*, starring Tatum O'Neal and Kristy McNichol. I had to keep the volume low as I sat in the middle of the living room floor. I don't even remember the movie now, because what happened was so deeply startling that everything else faded away. I laughed out loud at a funny scene. It was probably a bit of a squeal like many young girls make.

I was facing the TV when I heard my dad shoot straight up from his nap. I knew he was angry and immediately felt guilty, fully expecting to be yelled at. Instead, I heard, "What the hell is wrong with you?"

But it wasn't his voice—it was in my head. Maybe it was my own voice. I wasn't sure if it was real. I glanced back over my shoulder and saw he was sitting up looking irritated, but he was not talking. He was not even looking directly at me. In my mind, I said, "I'm sorry, Daddy!" Then I heard, "What was that about?" I again answered in my mind. "I'm sorry, it's the movie. There was a funny part, and I forgot you were sleeping." To which I immediately followed up with, "Is this real? Are we really talking in my head?" He answered, "What do you think?" We continued for a few minutes back and forth. I was stunned and in awe.

I had completely stopped watching the movie by that time but continued to stare directly at the TV. The conversation concluded with me saying, "Wow. This is so cool. I'm sorry I woke you." He responded, "Next time, try not to laugh so loud." He laid back down, and a short time later, my mom came in to tell us dinner was ready.

There were a few other random instances over the next five years, but nothing compared to that one clear conversation. My mom tells a story about when she was thinking about asking me to do something. I was in my bedroom listening to music, heard her call my name, and strolled down the hall to see what she wanted. She was surprised since she had not actually uttered a sound out loud.

The next full telepathic conversation I had with my dad was in the car when I was sixteen. A few days prior, I had told him I was pregnant. He decided the drive out of town for a family gathering would be the best time for me to tell my mom.

My boyfriend sat in the car next to me as my anxiety raged. I knew she would be disappointed. Thirty minutes into the drive, I heard my dad in my head once again. "Well, when are you going to tell her? Are you ready?"

"No, I don't think I will ever be ready. Can you help me start it?"

He then spoke out loud to prepare my mom. Afterward, I simply thought, "Thank you, Daddy."

He got back into my head. I silently asked him if he could read my thoughts. He responded, "When I want to." This was embarrassing. I was a teenager. I didn't want him to read my thoughts! I told him, "I don't want you in my head. I don't want you reading my mind." I was upset and told him to stay out. I began jumbling my thoughts intentionally. I quickly focused on sports, various types of food, cars on the highway, tying my shoes—whatever I could to throw him off the deep personal information. I successfully put up a mental wall to block him. Or maybe he just backed out. I could not have my father, the man I respected more than anyone, knowing my every thought. Life went on, and I ignored all those experiences. I didn't tell anyone for fear of being excluded from my inner circle and labeled crazy.

Have You Ever Been in a Crisis and Heard a Voice So Loudly, You *Had to Take Action?*

I witnessed my dad coming very near to death once. It involved a grand mal seizure, which led to therapy afterward. It was a horrible sight. Miraculously, he recovered, despite the doctors' predictions. One Thursday morning, thirteen years later, I got a call from my mom. She sleeps very late in the morning, but this time when she got up, my dad wasn't awake yet, which was very unusual. She told me he was speaking gibberish she could not understand. I knew it was another stroke. I had just dropped my husband off at the airport and was about ninety minutes from home. My brother-in-law was at a job site an hour away. My earth angel (my sister-in-law), who had joined our family through marriage a few years prior, was my only call. She and my brother-in-law lived next door to my parents. I called her and asked her to go over to help my mom, while I quickly got on the interstate and headed home.

I'm not sure of all that happened after that. Someone told me she was there and gave me the update, including that my dad was trying to go out the back door and was speaking unintelligibly. We all knew he did not want the paramedics called, as he had made clear after some recent falls. I drove ninety miles per hour to help. I think they were trying to get him dressed to take him to the hospital. I don't remember much of the drive. It was like Spirit was with me, clearing the path. About twenty minutes into the drive, I heard quite loudly, *Call the ambulance. They can't see what you saw.* A flash of his past stroke and seizure came to mind. I knew, like I knew, like I knew this was an absolute warning. I'm not sure what Spirit would have done had I not taken action. There was never a question in my mind.

I contacted my sister-in-law and gave the order to call the paramedics. I'm not sure if I gave a reason or if she even questioned me. I'm not sure how they got him onto the gurney and into the ambulance. What I know is that Spirit was right. I am grateful I got the message. Once at the hospital, the lead paramedic approached my mom to explain the delay in her getting to go in with my dad. Exactly three minutes after they loaded him onto the ambulance, he had a massive seizure and they intubated him. We all knew what the outcome would be and made the tough decisions that come with being a family. He passed away a few days later (though I'd rather say that he transitioned, since he simply changed energy and moved onto another dimension most of us cannot see).

The point is that Spirit was so incredibly loud and direct that I could not mistake the message for anything else. They had to call the ambulance so they would not have to endure the trauma of witnessing such a terrible event. There was absolutely no question in my mind about what was going to happen, and they would not be able to recover. Spirit intervened, and we are all grateful.

Have You Ever Inexplicably Known Something without a Single Doubt, with Every Fiber of Your Being?

Did you know it without even knowing how you knew it? One of my mentors says, "Know like you know like you know," and there really is no other description. For me it is something that is almost innate. You don't know how you know, but it is simply undeniable. Others may not believe you, but you are not swayed or able to be gaslit because you know it in your soul, with your entire being.

When I was eighteen, I went to real estate school to become a Realtor. One must pass the state exam to be licensed, and this was a challenge for me. At the end of the course, we had to pass a class exam intended to prepare us for the state exam. Then we had to wait several weeks until the state exam was scheduled. During those weeks, I put the books down and tended to my toddler and family. The test date had been set, and I had the class binders on the counter to review regularly … which I never did.

A week before the test date, I opened the binder. Disinterested, I closed it without studying. I decided I would cram for the test the day before. I was anxious about passing the state exam, which played a role in my avoidance of studying. If I failed, I would have to wait an entire month to retake it. The tests weren't scored immediately; they were submitted, and two to three weeks later the results would arrive in the mail (this was long before any virtual testing).

Days passed. When the night before the exam came. I put the binder on the dining room table and prepared to study all night, but I could not bring myself to sit in the chair and open the binder. I'm not sure how it happened or when I realized it was happening, but I found myself talking to someone—a being who was not visible to me and whom I had never met in this lifetime. He had passed away several years before I was born. I knew like I knew like I *knew* that I was talking to my paternal grandfather. I had a complete knowingness of his presence.

I was almost in tears, full of anxiety and guilt at not wanting to open that binder and study. As I became aware of our conversation, I said, "I don't want to study." In a firm and reassuring tone, my grandfather said, "Then don't. You already know the information." It almost felt like I was simply giving myself an out, but I absolutely knew it wasn't me. I asked him to help me pass the exam and be there with me to give me the answers if I got stuck. He agreed.

Early the next morning, I drove to the testing site two hours away. In a large lecture room, I sat in the top row with pencil and paper in hand. My grandfather was right. As I read the questions, I did know the answers! I read through the questions one by one and filled in the little oval next to the answer I believed to be correct. Any questions I didn't immediately know I left unanswered until I finished the ones I knew; this was a timed exam, and I knew this was the smartest testing strategy.

After the first run through, I turned back to the beginning, feeling a loving presence near me. I pondered the questions and completed a few answers before coming upon one that completely stumped me. I drew a complete blank. I closed my eyes and mentally said, "OK, Grandpa, this is where I need you." The next thing I knew, I was walking down the steps to submit the test. Three weeks later, I got the results in the mail. I passed the test and was granted the state license a few weeks later.

To this day, I still credit the grandfather I never knew. I have no doubt it was him calming me the night before and helping me pass the exam. I know like I know like I know.

Have You Ever Met a Person Who Glows and Exudes Love?

Maria is the type of person who silently walks into a room and whose energy brightens and fills the entire space. Her eyes sparkle brilliantly. Her genuine love for humanity just pours out of her. Even if you don't normally see auras, Maria's love energy is so palpable, you can feel it and literally see a glow surrounding her.

One could assume she is only out in public when she is in a blissful state, but in more than twenty-five years of friendship, I have seen her go through very difficult experiences. Even then, the true authentic energy of her heart was present in her aura. Her vibration is so high that every living thing can sense her loving energy. I know only one other such person. Interestingly, during some of my intense struggles, one of these two souls was present each step of the way. When I refer to my earth angels, these are the two I can easily identify in my life.

Have You Ever Known There Is a Soul Connection?

After several years with no connection, Maria and I met up for a business meeting one day. We were running through topics at warp speed without sticking to any one of them for more than a few minutes. We tried to focus on the priority because our time was limited. As we waited for her oil change to be finished, we finalized the next action steps for us to move forward in listing my mom's rental house for sale.

We continued to chat effortlessly. A recent trip to Las Vegas for Maria's granddaughter's dance competition. The latest book she'd read in her book club. Our love for our reliable SUVs. How many cup holders I needed in the front seats. We never took a breath, jumping from one thing to another without a single thought.

As you mature, you realize there are special types of friends. The true friends you have had for what seems like forever and really have a heart connection to are usually only a handful, and they are a gift to cherish. I have many casual friendships, but the type of friend I am talking about here is the one where you can go years without speaking or connecting in any way, then when you do connect, it was like you saw each other last week. Your souls are connected. My friend Maria is one of those special friends. We are like-minded and our friendship takes zero effort because it is sustained with pure love.

I can feel it. Maria is a special blessing and has had a huge impact on my spiritual journey. In fact, Maria, along with another close friend of ours, is who convinced me to begin reading spiritual books after college. I was an avid nonreader. I used my lack of time as an excuse, the same way one does to avoid going to the gym or exercising.

After suggesting a specific book on three separate occasions, I took their advice. The final convincing point was when Maria promised it was an "easy read." I remember exactly where we were and what we were doing. Back then, audiobooks were available, but we were still in the era of converting over our entire mindset to the digital world. I went to the local bookstore and bought the book. Immediately I noticed it was small and felt empowered to complete it. As promised, it was an easy read. *The Four Agreements* was one baby step along my spiritual growth journey. It fell in line with my beliefs and what I had studied in college. I think I learned true compassion from that book (which I highly recommend to anyone looking for any kind of personal growth). It really opened my eyes to awaken. Although I'm not sure when or where that awakening truly began.

The Universe has a path for us. Destiny. Fate. God's plan. We have reasons to be here in this lifetime. So many reasons that it is beyond comprehension. A significant purpose. Every person you have any type of relationship with is part of a greater purpose. It could be a lesson for you. It could be a lesson for them. It might just be a kind of connect-the-dots to another person. Or it might not be about you at all. It might be for them (remember this when connecting with others in a store or restaurant). You have an impact on every human being you connect with. A simple smile or sending energetic love could be exactly what that person needs for their purpose.

Looking back through this life, it is interesting to track where my spiritual journey opened up. My yoga guru once assigned our class to make a basic timeline and encouraged us to dig deeper into it in our future studies—another valuable piece of advice. Simply connecting the dots to Maria is an obvious path set by the Universe. I met Maria through working for Wilma, who would become a friend and mentor. I got the job working for her through my childhood and closest friend, who—you guessed it—is the very special soul whom I now refer to as "my spiritual bestie." Ironically—or not—she is also the person who connected me to the path to write this book. Her presence in my life is quite obviously part of my purpose here.

There is an undeniable soul connection.

Kendra Bergman

Mindfulness Exercise | *Connecting the Dots*

First, find a comfortable space and take a few breaths to quiet the mind. Close your eyes and ponder how you were led to read this book. Who or what is the reason you are reading it? Who or what event led you here? As the answer comes to you, open your eyes, and write it on the lines below.

_____

_____

_____

_____

_____

_____

_____

_____

_____

_____

_____

_____

Now, ponder where and how that person or event came into your life. Who or what preceded it that led you here? Continue to connect the dots back as far as you can. It might be two steps, or it might be twenty. Write in each one as you remember each event or person.

_____

_____

_____

_____

_____

_____

_____

_____

_____

_____

Example for how I was led to write this book, working backward:

- A session with the Angel Medium
- Scheduled session after hearing *Angels & Awakening Podcast* #291, "Your 2022 Forecast and Messages from Spirit"
- Led to podcast by spiritual bestie
- Met her at church youth group at age fourteen
- Led to church youth group by high school classmates (Thank you, Tanya and Lisa!)

Janet Ciarvella, age 67

I had the privilege of being the caregiver for a beautiful lady named Mary Brown. She was a very elegant woman who always had her hair done, her makeup on, and was dressed "to the nines." Even when she was in the hospital, she would apply her orange lipstick—her favorite color.

Following a dangerous fall, Mary was placed in hospice care, and we were able to tend to her at her home. As she neared the end of her life, we often played music for her (usually big band, which was her favorite). As I sat with Mary, music playing softly, I could sense the presence of her late husband in the room along with other friends and family who had passed. There was a sense of her group of friends gathering around the foot of her bed, waiting for her to cross over. To my surprise, it was a party-like atmosphere!

As Mary lay there, still physically present in her earthly body, I could feel that she was waiting for her favorite nighttime caregiver to come say his goodbyes. He arrived about thirty minutes later. Shortly after, I began to pray the rosary for her, as was her custom. I looked at her face and she started to glow. Her aged skin became so soft, and her wrinkles faded. She was youthful and newly vibrant. I quickly called her daughter to come into the room and asked her what she saw. We both stood in awe as we watched Mary's face glowing and radiating right in front of us. Slowly, the glow left her face and then rose into the upper corner of the wall and disappeared.

The music abruptly stopped. I sensed that the passed-on family and friends who'd just previously surrounded her bed were gone. The party was over, and Mary had gone to be with her husband and friends. The room felt empty. Lynn and I looked at each other. We hugged, cried, and laughed.

Another Dimension: The Other Side

Be curious, not judgmental.
—Walt Whitman

For a long time, I knew my beliefs did not fit in with any of the traditional religions. My parents encouraged spiritual growth in many ways. They allowed me to attend a variety of Christian churches growing up. I have always believed in God. I have read the Bible. I read it with an open mind, open enough to understand that many written texts can be perceived differently by different people. When I began studying philosophy in college, it started to click. God, also called Source, the Divine, or various other titles, does exist. There is another side. There is heaven. There are other dimensions. We know the difference now between two dimensions and three dimensions. I have seen recent references to the fourth and fifth dimensions and made a mental note to read about them. I refer to it as the Other Side. It can be heaven, it can be a place between our earthly life and heaven, it can even be another planet, or perhaps it is the sun or another star. Wherever it is, it is beyond human earthly life because our souls continue to live on. The energy of our soul does not die. It transcends into another energetic form and moves to the other side.

We each have an entire team of spirits and angels to guide us through this lifetime. They are on a different plane or dimension, on the other side. They are with us as we awaken to find the path of true enlightenment, which may take several earthly lifetimes. They love, protect, and guide us. God, angels, spirit guides, and loved ones who have passed all make up our spirit team.

As humans all around the world are awakening; we are realizing it is natural to feel the energies around us. Those who dared to challenge the stigma of craziness and passed down the awareness and acceptance of seeing spirits, angels, or loved ones through the generations have made an impact. We have now seen enough movies and read enough books for much of the population to accept and rediscover their spiritual gifts. As we begin to awaken our consciousness, we must do our own research.[3] We can dive into podcasts, books, YouTube videos, and movies that resonate with our true selves.

Gifts

Everyone has special gifts. Some may simplify it into intelligence, talent, or personality traits. You probably know someone who is especially good with numbers. They can calculate things in their head whereas it would take someone else five steps on a calculator. Or they can remember phone numbers, addresses, bank account numbers, and more without writing them down. You may know someone who is an artist. You may have experienced a connection with someone who you can actually *feel* their healing touch. These are not skills which are learned from a class or teaching institution. They are gifts. Have you identified and developed your gifts? Perhaps you have a spiritual gift and do not even realize it yet.

It may go even deeper as you contemplate it. Do you find yourself seeing, hearing, feeling, or getting a sense of knowingness about things? What is your unique, God-given spiritual gift?

---

[3] See pages 73-74 for more recommendations.

Julie Jancius says, "Some people call themselves Intuitives. They may not know where the information they are receiving is coming from. It may be from a collective group of beings who are connected through God's white light and may not be from a particular loved one, angel or guide."

Who Are You Asking?

How many times do you ask yourself, *What is that word? How do I spell that? Where did I put that?* Listen to your questions throughout the day. When the answer comes to you, where do you think it comes from? When you ask the question, remember that it is your spirit team whispering in your ear. Sometimes they don't know the answer, or your frequency is not tuned into the correct energy station, so to speak. It doesn't mean they are not there; it simply means they aren't able to give it to you. But what about when they do? You hear it or know it somehow. It comes to your brain. How did it get there?

Think about a time you have asked yourself a question. A simple one. *Do I want a burger or chicken? Should I wear jeans or dress pants? Should I try to go back to sleep or just get up two hours early?* It is absolutely natural. Now, when you have those questions, consider who you are asking. The automatic response is *myself*. Reflect on that response. Why would you ask yourself a question? If you are asking yourself, wouldn't you already know the answer?

Sometimes the answers come to us before we are even finished with the question.

Universe, Source, Spirit Team, God, Angels—all the energies who are with us can answer instantaneously when we are tuned into the correct frequency, because our mind works faster than we realize. Sometimes the answers aren't simple, and it may take a while for reasons we do not understand. *Where did I leave my keys?* may take time to answer. Perhaps you are not open to hearing the answer. They may guide you to look here or there. Or perhaps you misplaced them because Spirit knew you needed to be delayed by two minutes to avoid a tragic accident that would have been on your path. Maybe it wasn't even for you. The accident could have been disrupting someone else's destiny. Do you ever get in the car to go somewhere and become aware you are coming to almost every red light on your path? Consider that it may be divine intervention. Things happen all throughout the day that we are oblivious to. We don't realize the purpose because we are so busy trying to get somewhere or get something accomplished, and then the egoic mind steps in and takes over. Therefore, taking just a few minutes for meditation and prayer are so important. When we quiet our egoic mind, we may get an inexplicable knowingness of things or even see, hear, or feel things. Perhaps they are ideas to guide humanity into the future or experiences for us to learn from or share with close friends.

Mindfulness Exercise | *Breathe in the Present Moment*

Find a quiet space to settle in and make some time to be still. As you become aware of your thoughts, begin to focus your attention on the following affirmations:

My body and breath anchor me to the here and now.
My internal experiences do not control me. I am their observer.
I can choose how I respond to my thoughts.
I can observe the sensations I feel. I can see past them.

Repeat them quietly to yourself for five to ten minutes. When you're ready, take a moment to describe how you feel and anything you heard or saw in your mind's eye.

_____

_____

_____

_____

_____

_____

_____

_____

_____

Danelle Poe, age 50

In 2019, I would drive from Sierra Vista, Arizona, to Tucson every day—my father was dealing with the side effects of his cancer treatments. On the road from Tucson back to Sierra Vista, the drive is partially flat land and partially mountainous. One day, while I was driving back home on Interstate 10, I came up on a semitruck passing another semitruck. I hesitated because my father was a retired Arizona Highway Patrolman / State Trooper who had taught me to be careful around these trucks. "You don't want to get yourself stuck between them," he'd say. With no other vehicles coming, I got into the left lane to also pass the semi.

The semi I was behind was taking a lot longer than I had estimated to pass the semi in the right lane. I could see that we were approaching a large hill between mountains. My father would say, "Always be aware of your surroundings—look in those mirrors." I saw another semitruck coming up behind me. As we got closer to the hill, I could see that he was coming up quickly. As we went up the hill between the mountains, he came up so fast behind me that I had to jerk my steering wheel to the left toward the mountainside. The semitruck that was now behind my 4Runner was going to have me crushed in the middle of all these enormous eighteen-wheelers. I looked back within seconds and saw the semi that was about to hit me was now in the right lane. I blinked because I could not believe my eyes.

I looked to the right of me, and that same semi had now moved up in the right lane. There is no way that this could have happened. Immediately I knew I had just experienced divine intervention. My mind raced as I thought of angels, then I thought, *Did my husband's father, who is on the other side, have a hand along with angels?* It was as if time changed in just seconds, but I couldn't rationalize how it had happened in my human mind. Did they pick up my truck and move me, move the eighteen-wheelers? I just did not know. What I *did* know without a doubt is that I had help from the other side. My spirit team knew that my emotions, mind, and heart were somewhere else while my dad was struggling, and so they stepped in; for that I am beyond thankful.

I'd had earlier experiences and had been communicating with the Other Side for quite a while by that point. To this day, I consider myself a student and know that I need to share what I have learned spiritually in order to help others. This was one of many events in my life that I thank my spirit team for.

For God may speak in one way, or in another, yet man does not perceive it. In a dream, in a vision of the night, when deep sleep falls upon men, while slumbering on their beds, then He opens the ears of men, and seals their instruction. (Job 33:14–16 NKJV)

Communicating with Your Spirit Team

Many years ago, I heard Oprah refer to "God whispers" or "aha moments." It made perfect sense to me—whatever we call it, it's our spirit team sending us messages. You could be hearing angels, spirit guides, or loved ones who have passed to the other side. You are reading this book because you have been called to question what you are hearing, seeing, feeling, or getting a sense of knowingness. You are tuned in to a frequency connected with a source of a higher power: God, angels, universe, spirit, the divine, higher self, source.

Whatever you believe in, you know in your heart of hearts there is a higher power than humans.

We can commune with our spirit team during prayer and meditation. When we quiet our mind, sit, or lie in stillness and give them our undivided attention, they are with us to answer our call. The question is, how do we understand their responses and truly receive their messages? Many people pray only when they are in the worst circumstances. The Universe doesn't wave a magic wand to make all our challenges disappear simply because we ask. We have lessons to learn in this earthly lifetime. If we pay attention, we will have the answers and guidance we need, even if it doesn't match what we want or think we need at that moment.

Meeting My Spirit Guides

It isn't as much of a meeting with the guides and angels as it is getting to know them. They are always with us, even if we don't acknowledge their presence. As humans do, once I recognize a voice or an energy of a specific angel or guide, I want to identify it with a name and image. Although I realize these beings are an energy field, I continue to look for identifying visual features. Then I want to "put a name with the face." According to my "sarcastic guide," this is nonsense and unnecessary.

In the early 2000s I had enough spiritual knowledge and mentoring to decide I wanted to "meet" my spirit guides. One of my most influential teachers had told me they often come in at early hours of the morning. The energy surrounding the physical location is calm and less chaotic. Your egoic mind is quiet. I filed the information away, knowing I would someday need to remember it.

A few years went by as our life often does. Then, in early 2006, I reconnected with the same spiritual teacher in an abstract art and painting class. As I painted, I felt the peaceful presence of guides and angels. I began going to sleep every night with the hope and invitation of meeting one of my guides. I put the energetic thought out there to the Universe, similar to a prayer.

Bellulah

One night, probably weeks later, I woke up around two o'clock in the morning. As I attempted to drift back to sleep, I fell into a dreamlike state, in a space between being awake and asleep. A state of awakened consciousness. I met my first known spirit guide as I walked into a kitchen. Her name is Bellulah, although the name did not come right away. Even now, I can recall the image of that first meeting clearly. She was on the other side of the counter as I entered and sat down on a barstool. The kitchen area was open air, yet somehow indoors. For a while, I sat, not saying anything but feeling the sense of awe of her physical presence as I took it all in.

She is a Black woman with a distinct fruit basket on her head. The fruit basket doesn't move. I'm not even sure if it is real or plastic fruit.

It is strikingly beautiful and belongs with her as if it were a part of her body. She is very kind and reassuring. Not chatty, but there to give advice or ease my worries.

As I sat, I asked who she was. She looked up at me from her chopping and smiled with an expression that said, "you already know." So, I said, 'You're my spirit guide." She nodded yes. "Do you have a name?" Again, she grinned with an "of course" expression. This is where I learned she is not talkative. Her presence is a calming motherly presence. In many of the moments when I am consciously aware of spending time with my guides, there is very little of what I would call communication. It is difficult to describe.

I sat quietly, watching her chop vegetables. She kept smiling and occasionally looked up lovingly at me. After a period of what seemed like five minutes, I asked her differently. "What is your name?" The answer was given to me, although not spoken. It wasn't entirely clear. It became almost a knowingness of a word without understanding it. Finally, I put it together and got the whole word out. "Bellulah." She spoke for the first time, saying, "Yes, child. You can call me Bellulah." I quietly got up from the stool as she came around the side of the counter wiping her hands on her apron and opening her arms to give me the biggest hug I ever had. I felt like a little girl in her arms. It was incredibly comforting. I thanked her for meeting with me and turned around to walk out as I came out of the dream state. It was an experience I am still very grateful for.

Chin

Chin appeared shortly afterward. One night before falling asleep I realized my mind was in another place. Somewhere I have never been physically, nor do I recall seeing it on TV or anywhere else. It was like I was drawn there for quiet time to reflect. I was sitting on a wooden bench on a wooden deck near a stream, surrounded by pure beauty. As I tuned into the place, I noticed that a reassuring presence (being) was sitting next to me in complete stillness and silence.

I sat and took in all the serenity around me. After a few moments, I turned toward the male energy. I caught a glimpse of a figure with a distinctive red hat. He was wearing a red robe with gold lettering over red pants in an Asian-inspired outfit. The brim of the hat came down over his eyes, appearing to be lowered in contemplation. It had gold lettering written in a language I did not recognize.

The first time I saw his eyes was in a painting I created in our abstract art class. Each week my mom, sister, and I would bring our piece home for our husbands to evaluate. We would all stand around and share what we saw in it. Some of the art was better than others, to say the least. I had completed one piece, with which I wasn't particularly fond of the results. So, I considered painting over the canvas. I decided to sit with it for a while and hung it on the wall.

Then one night, I was looking at it and noticed that distinctive hat shape over his nose and his sweet smile. The brim of the hat was up just enough so I could see his eyes. It was Chin's face in the upper corner looking down at the rest of the painting in a protective way. The painting happens to be of outer space with a planet in the front center. There is no doubt in the message that he is in the heavens watching me. The painting now hangs on the wall near my bed. When I need comfort, I look up at the face to feel him near me. Sometimes I look at it with no intention or conscious thought, which will remind me to close my eyes, sit on the deck, and just be.

When I could mentally "see" him and the place he lived, I found myself visiting regularly. At some point I was able to understand his name, even though our communication was limited. This is the place of solitude and comfort. I often visit after a stressful day or when I have a problem to solve. I don't know when or how I realized the way to get to him, but it was a short journey once I closed my eyes.

I could walk there in my mind's eye. I walk along a path next to a fence until I see the stream. I continue walking until I come to the beautiful wooden bridge over the stream. I pause at the center of the bridge, and I look over the railing into the flowing stream. It is filled with koi fish and greenery like lily pads. This is where I leave the chaos behind. It is a knowingness. If I cross the bridge, I must sit quietly and be still. Present. I know Chin is there.

I am not allowed to bring any hyped-up energy over. I turn to see Chin on the deck near the other side of the bridge and walk forward, free from my stressful thoughts. Sometimes when I am mentally wound up about something, I will walk down the path before I go to sleep. I've realized the walks are sometimes longer than others. I can see him sitting on the deck, basking in the beauty and silence. If I rush, I end up walking farther. The path goes on and on. As I settle, the bridge appears and the fence ends. We simply sit.

After sitting with Chin several times, I opened my eyes wider and turned to notice the surroundings. I noticed that his house (which may have been a study or a porch area), is open air like in the *Karate Kid* movie. It has a long, wooden wraparound deck with red and gold lanterns hanging down. The colors are beautiful with dark wood, plants and greenery, and the lanterns mixed in.

I was fascinated by my surroundings. Each time I was there, I would look around to see whatever I could in an attempt to understand Chin, his history, and his purpose in my life. I wanted to remember every detail in some kind of false hope that I would know all there is about him. The human curiosity factor I suppose. My interest in his home and surroundings continue to this day. Every now and then I can look around and add another piece of the visual picture.

Over the years, we have had some brief conversations. It usually involves me asking questions and him looking at me with the brim of his hat almost covering his eyes or placing his hand on top of mine. With Chin, I rarely hear any words. It is more like I just know or get the message somehow. I have come to learn this is normal for many people. I will often say or write that I "heard" a message. Some of my angels and guides speak with words I can interpret; others I just have the message via a knowingness. Chin transmits the messages in a knowingness way. However, when I ask him questions, he does not always answer. Mostly he sits quietly, urging me to do the same. When he does answer a question, it is usually brief, profound, and calming. Several times I have sat next to him and cried. He simply pats my hand for comfort.

I recall a point in time when I felt particularly lost and frustrated in my everyday life. I hesitated to visit because I knew I was carrying a heavy energetic load. As I took the steps up the deck, he patted the seat next to him and said the first word I have ever heard him speak. "Sit." He spoke in such a calm, sweet, yet commanding tone of voice. As usual, we just sat there. This time I didn't try to look around. I didn't try to observe and record every detail of my surroundings. I sat in peace. Occasionally I would begin to look at him to ask a question, and I would hear a "shhhhhh" sound.

For a long time, we did not speak. We sat quietly until my impatient mind finally asked, "When can I leave?" He didn't answer at first. We sat in silence again. Finally, I knew the answer. I could stand up and walk back over that bridge any time I wanted. I recall wondering why he rarely spoke. The knowingness I had afterward was more of a sense than can be truly described. I knew I was meant to simply be still. It is a place of peace—a place to observe the beauty all around us.

I understand his purpose on my spirit team. He is what I consider my guide of quietude and comfort. I haven't sat with him much in several years but have "heard" I need to visit him more often.

Jedi Bob

I have already mentioned a "sarcastic guide" who has been with me for many years. I easily recognize his tone and his energy. After getting to know Bellulah and Chin with visual images and a name, I was finally able to get a vision of this guide. He is a tall, thin Black man. He is draped in a tan fabric covering, much like a toga. I sense he is from the desert, or some other place of pure sand. His personality is much more identifiable than an image. He is absolutely the humorous guide. My best friend, who doesn't sugarcoat anything. He's the one who gives me the tough messages. He often will pop up with "duh" or "of course" when I am considering something. He is a strong, undeniable personality. Gathering a name from him was a different kind of challenge, but it finally happened during that meditation in the hospital.

Mindfulness Exercise | *Gratitude for Your Guides*

Find a quiet and comfortable space where you can settle for a while and truly ground yourself. Start this exercise by writing to your guides for one minute, expressing your gratitude for their guidance in your life. Take one more minute to ask them any questions weighing on your heart. Take two or three minutes to write down any insight that comes forward (and if that insight comes later in the day, week, or month, remember you can always return to this page or your own journal to note what your guides shared with you).

_____

_____

_____

_____

_____

_____

_____

_____

_____

_____

_____

Meditation and Journaling Benefits

Brilliant things happen in calm minds ...
—Russell Glass

Consider the benefits of meditation. Why are meditation and prayer so important? Meditating allows us to raise our vibrational energy to tune into the higher self and listen to God and our entire spirit team. You close out the chaos of every moment of constant doing and quiet yourself to connect. Prayer is talking to your spirit team. Meditation is quieting the mind to listen to them. Think about all the times you were able to truly feel whatever was going on, emotionally and physically. When you are down on your knees praying, you and your thoughts are quiet, like when you are meditating.

Do you hear messages when you are in the shower, styling your hair, or doing dishes? It depends on what is going on around you, doesn't it? If you are jumping in the shower to rush off to begin the day, you may not pause to listen. If your kids are running around or asking homework questions while you are doing the dishes, there is no space to listen. We have become such an inundated society; we don't take the time to just be quiet. I know life is busy and hectic, but as I tell my meditation students, there is always time, even thirty seconds. Trust this. It is more important than most people realize.

Take time before going to sleep to scan your body and feel it. Address its needs or discomforts. Visualize pure health and vitality. Pause in the middle of the day to check in emotionally, mentally, and physically, even if this must be done while going to the bathroom—at least give yourself those few seconds to quiet the mind from all the other noise and to-dos.

Journaling to Tune In

In recent years, journaling has become a standard practice in our culture. Most adults over twenty-five know and understand what it is. We understand the logic of it and may have even experienced the success of it. If you journal daily, you are a success story. You are probably also more connected with your higher self than you realize. Journaling has existed since humans could write. It is a quiet time of connection; all the thoughts and messages we hear, but do not actually listen to, are flowing out freely. We share our emotions and thoughts and in doing so, we are connected. When we journal, we do not accuse ourselves of being crazy for hearing thoughts. Instead, we slow down the messages enough to process them.

Try journaling consistently for ten minutes every night before going to sleep. If you have nothing to write, try "I can't think of anything to write." But sit in the silence, notebook in hand, ready to write what does come to mind. Do this for at least seven days. Trust that you will have something to write. Maybe it's more than ten minutes. Maybe after you finish journaling for a few minutes you have a ton of thoughts—this is the other side speaking to you. You are not crazy. It could be God, angels, spirit guides, or loved ones from the other side. We all have the ability to tune into the other side to receive messages of guidance and love. Before we can tune it correctly, though, we must allow ourselves to believe things which are not easily understood.

Maria's Meditation

In less than an hour, Maria and I touched on numerous topics, including philosophical and controversial ones. One such topic was gender identification. We quickly engaged on common thoughts, when I mentioned wondering about the overall picture of how we, as humans, seem to be evolving into a unisex population, almost like the pictures of the gray aliens we see in movies. She agreed and shared a meditation experience confirming what we already know. Energy is energy. It may be masculine or feminine, but on the other side, energy does not identify. There is no suit of flesh as a human body.

Maria went on to describe a meditative experience she had that was so detailed, I could actually *see* it in my mind's eye. She referred to the meditation state as "going into the gap." This is what I think of as the other side. I don't know if it is another dimension or plane or perhaps planet, but it is in between our earthly presence and Heaven. I hadn't heard it referred to as "the gap," but I now realize it is the perfect description.

She saw genderless beings in shells. The best word to describe it was *auras*. I could see what she was describing. It's not uncommon to visualize something from the Other Side and not actually have a word to name it. Either way, whether it was a telepathic image she shared, or my own visualization, I saw what she described.

The beings Maria saw were everywhere. Some were standing or walking, and some were sitting. They were essentially lines of chakra energy colors. In my mind's eye, I saw white aura light surrounding a figure similar to a human shape. Then small balls of energetic colors lined up on the seven major chakra energy centers. There was a humanlike shape to the beings without any real identifying features. They all looked exactly the same, yet I knew they were many separate energetic beings. There were no furniture or plants. It was simply a blank area with veiled shapes surrounding a line of seven small, colored balls. The area was filled with the beings. They were almost floating since there were no surfaces to see as they sat, walked, and moved. The scene was magical. It probably lasted only a minute or two, but the vision had such an effect on me, it seemed time had stopped.

The experience was so intense that tears of love and knowingness came to my eyes. Her recall of her meditation was flawless. I felt as though I had been there with her. At some point, I remember thinking, *Wow* as I processed the overwhelming sense of fullness in my heart. After a brief pause, I asked her if I could put it in this book and she readily approved. Since we only had an hour together, I had barely mentioned I was writing a book. I'm sure coming from the woman she had to convince to read books, it was a notable celebration. She briefly shared my excitement, giving me a high five as we jumped to another topic.

I didn't get the chance to explain much about the book or my purpose for writing it. I summarized it in brief terms. The word "crazy" should be eliminated as a quantifier as a belief or opinion. As a society, we must begin to share our experiences and beliefs in order to stop the excessive self-doubting. Realizing there are many other like-minded souls experiencing similar things will bring us together into Oneness, the powerful ultimate love energy. Every person is a tiny droplet of God, Source, Universe, The Divine—all the above. Loving, positive experiences and beliefs do not classify anyone as insane.

The Wellness Connection

Always hold fast to the present. Every situation, indeed every moment, is of infinite value, for it is the representative of the whole eternity.
—Johann Wolfgang von Goethe

Any one aspect of our life affects the others. For example, when our physical health is in jeopardy, it takes a toll on our mental, emotional, and spiritual health as well. It is our responsibility to connect with our spirit team regularly to keep ourselves on track and in complete health. Sometimes it can be a difficult lesson and can take a lot of work to get it all flowing again.

If life was easy, there would be no lessons to learn. As humans, we would not be driven to develop our personal and spiritual growth. The messages and lessons I received in the hospital room meditation were powerful, but once I was discharged, I had to do the work of figuring out how to implement them into my actual life. The first challenge was recovering. Thanks to the two-by-four, I had been forced into a situation where there were no other options except to focus on my physical health. Did I process payroll from my hospital bed against my doctor's wishes? Yes. Did I continue to struggle daily to perform necessary tasks as the CEO of a business? Yes. However, what I was forced to do was to minimize my business work to only the absolute necessities. I did the tasks that could only be done by me. Coaching and teaching other people became the work priority. Letting go of control was the most difficult process for me.

I am incredibly blessed and grateful to have a husband and family who have always been amazingly supportive. Long before I fell ill, I'd known my husband was a generous man. I rarely cooked, cleaned, shopped, or washed laundry since he had retired from his first career years prior, and he took on even more after that scary day. My mom, whom I had been visiting at least four days a week to assist with paperwork from my dad's death, help with her bills, accompany her to appointments, and schedule home maintenance, did not ask me to come over or help except on very rare occasions. She even offered to take me to appointments and bring us food. My brother-in-law and sister-in-law spent even more time with my mom than they already had to ease my concerns over her care and companionship.

Physically, healing and recovering was a long process. Since I had let several years pass without seeing a doctor, I had to choose a new primary care physician before leaving the hospital. The hospital staff scheduled the follow-up appointment for me. When I first saw her, she spent three hours with me thoroughly going over my hospital records. For more than a year, she guided me every step of the way toward recovery. At one of the follow-ups several weeks after discharge, she limited me to doing one thing a day. See, even though I had been given the signs and experienced the unthinkable, my personality traits did not change. All the things I had been tending to before I was hospitalized did not go away. I improved at delegating and releasing control over many things, but I continued to push myself further than my body was prepared for.

Mentally, I thought I would bounce back quickly. My doctor counseled me numerous times on the traumatic experience my body went through, which would take time to heal. Patience is a trait I am still working to improve to this day. After two months of setbacks, I followed doctor's orders. My memory was shot, a common side effect of sepsis. To ensure I didn't forget or commit to too many things in a day, I scheduled one activity per day in my phone calendar. If I had any kind of appointment, that would be all for the day. The rest of the day would be designated to rest. If I had a class or workshop to attend, I would plan a day before leaving and at least one day after for rest and recovery. If I was teaching a one-hour yoga class, the rest of the day was spent in bed. If someone asked me to do anything, I would intentionally check my calendar before answering and immediately put it in my phone when I did commit. Once I let go of the need to control my body's timeline of recovery, I gradually improved.

I had to accept that I would be different from what I was before sepsis. No matter how supportive they were, the fact of the matter was that friends and family did not experience the same awareness of my decline as I did. At one point, a year later, my husband tried to console me as I complained and teared up with frustration at not being able to calculate math in my head. He said, "Honey, a lot of people can't do that." I said, "It's not that I can't do it that upsets me. It's that I can't do it *anymore*." I realized in that moment that I might never be able to do the things I did previously. However, I could accept and cherish the new person I am with the things I am able to do and the new things I will learn. I frequently used the phrase *It is what it is* to cope and ground myself. It was a roller coaster ride, but my family and friends held my hand through every turn. By letting go of self-imposed expectations and focusing on my spiritual health, my emotional health improved.

Prior to my NDE, I had developed a good spiritual practice using many tools: gratitude, positive words and thoughts, meditation, prayer, journaling, kindness to others and myself, and sharing universal love energy. As I entrenched myself in necessary tasks and accomplishments, I lost my sense of priority and dropped several of the keys to my own spiritual practice. I had the tools to maintain each aspect of my health, but I did not prioritize using them. Instead, I took my spiritual health for granted. I used "life happens" as an excuse to procrastinate about maintaining any sort of a healthy lifestyle because I knew it would be temporary. I knew I was strained emotionally and mentally, which I also realized could be taxing on my physical well-being. I simply did not understand the concept of spiritual health, which is why I continued to put off my spiritual practice—it seemed the least important.

In hindsight, if I'd taken a few minutes every day to meditate and commune with my spirit team, I might have realized the temporary strain that had gone on for too long. If you remember nothing else from this book, remember that spiritual practice is of utmost importance. It is called a *practice* because it will never be perfect (which we must accept). We are in a constant state of practice to develop, learn, and continually improve. After the hospital meditation, I renewed my commitment and continue to pursue more knowledge, awareness, and awakening.

> **Knowing yourself is the beginning of all wisdom.**
>
> **—Aristotle**

It's All Connected

Sometimes I think people depend on me. Sometimes I think I can take on the world by myself. Sometimes I think I can do it all. My wise cousin once told me, "You need to be needed. You *want* to be needed."

She is right. I think we all do. It's human nature, whether we're needed to feed the dog, water the garden, cook for friends and family, or talk to a loved one. Most of us forget to set boundaries or do things in moderation. We may put self-care as a last priority.

My generation was taught to set life goals, career goals, personal goals, family goals—goals. Where do you want to be in six months? One year? Five years? Ten years? Goals are productive, but only if you manage your expectations of yourself. Many people (including me) tend to put so much pressure on ourselves to be "somewhere" and accomplish "something" by certain milestones that we often lose sight of what is going on in the present moment—the Now.

I remember feeling disappointed in myself on my twenty-fifth birthday. I was depressed, but it turned out to be one of the best phases of my life. I had subconsciously set unreasonable expectations for myself. Expectations are different from goals: Expectations are an absolute belief that something will be achieved or accomplished. Goals are an aim or intent to achieve something. I had been comparing myself to what other people I admired had accomplished by the time they were twenty-five. But my life journey was different, and for that, I am incredibly grateful.

It is a journey. It is about learning lessons and appreciating the good times along with the tough times. We take various turns, go over bumps, and get stuck in the mud, but the Universe always guides us back to the path for our destiny. Regardless of how determined or focused we are on something we feel must be done, the Universe guides us back. That guidance can be gentle if we are open and aware, or it can be a two-by-four if we are stubborn and have tunnel vision.

The saying "hindsight is twenty-twenty" couldn't be more accurate. In 2015 I had been given so many signs to make changes. There were so many open doors and forks in the road to choose from, but I did not waiver. I was laser focused on what I *thought* was my path. I did not notice the doors, forks, signs, and opportunities until reflecting on why a two-by-four had hit me over the head.

On paper I looked great. I felt successful and important. I was CEO of a small business, on the executive board of a nonprofit, an active daughter of aging parents, and a world traveler, wife, mother, aunt, and friend. The practices of yoga and spirituality crossed my mind, but neither were a priority. I intended to get back into walking every day with my husband, but there weren't enough hours in the day to add it in and maintain all the other daily joys and commitments. My core became weaker and weaker as I did fewer physical activities each month. But I'd also allowed the core of my *being* to become weaker as time passed. I continued pushing myself in many different directions while ignoring my own spiritual and physical needs.

One weekend while rushing around, I moved some furniture to vacuum under it without thinking about my movements and strained my back. It was frustrating. I opted out of some activities with my husband and spent a few days nursing my lower back. Eventually it was time for me to suck it up and endure whatever discomfort I was feeling and go to work. There were important tasks that needed to be completed, and I was the only one who could complete them; at least that's what I thought. By the middle of the day, I bent over a file cabinet (once again in a rush) and that was it. The two-by-four this time was a herniated disc. I lay on the floor in pain, unable to get up. My spirit team had eliminated every distraction to force me to see that I could not do it all on my own. I needed help and the independence I prided myself on was no longer an option.

I eventually made it off the floor and was able to function, but the pain was unbearable. A father-son chiropractic team treated me twice a day, seven days a week for several weeks. I spent many hours in their office. Fortunately, they had a massage therapist on staff who specialized in injury recovery, and she also worked on me for months. I had to essentially stop working. I flew my son in from out of state to help with the business.

When we convince ourselves that we can handle all the different aspects of our lives alone, it is often an indicator that we need help. Many of us don't realize how many people are willing to help if we simply admit we need it and ask for it. An entire group of people I thought needed my help jumped in to help me. I have been blessed with so many family members and friends who are truly compassionate and generous.

That two-by-four moment was a big one. Its purpose was just to remind me I didn't have to set and meet unreasonable expectations for myself. It was also a roadblock that redirected me back onto the path of my soul's journey. The signs were there. I just did not prioritize self-care until I no longer had a choice.

In my professional and volunteer positions during the previous year, I had run into an old acquaintance several times. It did not seem important at the time. In hindsight, it was the opportunity and sign to take a different direction. I was supposed to make room in my life for spiritual and personal growth but was intent on professional success and making my family proud. This acquaintance was a licensed massage therapist who had transitioned into her own business. I remember taking her business card, intending to schedule a massage. Naturally, I did not make the time for it. A few months later, I saw her at another function. We had a few minutes to talk, and she mentioned she had become a yoga instructor. Again, I took her card intending to take classes *and* book a massage. I was intrigued by yoga. Many people think of it as the physical positions, or physical exercise, but I knew it was so much more. I wanted to delve into it and learn. I wanted to become more flexible, strengthen and tone my body and my inner core. I didn't call or make the time. The third time I saw her was shortly before my back injury. We discussed the days and times of her classes. I knew I could make at least one a week if I set aside the time. I didn't.

I was determined to heal without surgery. I hired an exercise coach with physical therapy experience who worked with me three times a week. I had a massage two times a week. I tried supplements, ice packs, nerve pain medications, rest, exercise, stretching, acupuncture, cortisone shots, and yes—finally made it to yoga. The instructor taught a gentle yoga class twice a week. After several months, I improved enough to function for several hours per day. I could work lying down while using a laptop. I was able to sit, stand, and walk if I used the pain medications and muscle relaxers. Through it all, I was diligent about attending yoga class twice a week, every week. But after a year, I realized I wanted more out of life than simply being able to function and began consulting with specialists and planned the surgery.

After the spinal fusion surgery, I expected four to six weeks of recovery. There were days I wondered if it worked. I followed the doctor's every instruction. But even six months later, the pain continued to be unbearable. The surgeon could only tell me that everyone recovered at different rates. Other than pain medications, which I tried to minimize, walking and gentle yoga were the only advice the specialists could offer. I expected a 100 percent recovery within twelve weeks at the most. But some days, I would notice small improvements in my strength and flexibility, and on other days I felt as though I had experienced an immense setback. Managing my own expectations is a work in process for me.

As I continued making the yoga classes a priority as part of my recovery, my teacher began to discuss how she got her certification and suggested I attend the same training school. I was hesitant but decided the advertised course of "200 hours teacher training and personal growth intensive" could only serve to benefit me. To my surprise, they accepted me into the course even though I was still recovering from back surgery with limited mobility. It was the decision my spirit team had been guiding me toward for years. During the two-month intensive training program, two important things occurred: my back pain subsided as my core strengthened, and I discovered that I enjoyed teaching yoga. I took the class for education and personal growth and completed it with an unexpected vocation.

Yoga saved me from a frightening and painful phase of my life. My spirit team hit me over the head with the two-by-four to realign my path toward my soul's purpose. The yoga teacher training program was the introduction to a new phase in my life I never thought I would have the time for. Personal and spiritual growth must be a priority in all our lives no matter how busy, driven, or determined we are to succeed in other aspects of our lives. It is all connected.

Kendra Bergman

Mindfulness Exercise | *Breathing Mindfully*

One common method of calming the nervous system, easing anxiety, and improving mental clarity is mindful breathing. This is done when you focus on your breath, breathing from your diaphragm at a steady pace for a set amount of time. When you're ready, take some time away in a quiet space to focus on your breath. You may even like to play some calming music, using it to keep your breathing at a rhythmic pace. Commit to this exercise for five to ten minutes or as long as you'd like. When you're ready, use the space provided to describe how you felt before and after this exercise.

_____

_____

_____

_____

_____

_____

_____

_____

_____

_____

Releasing the Fear
of Judgment

**To be unafraid of the judgment of others
is the greatest freedom you can have.**
—Timothy Shriver

Let go of the fear or concern of what others will think or say and share your experience or thoughts about spirituality or the other side. As you share your stories, you may find many others sharing similar ones. Many ideas have been considered impossible, outrageous, or taboo until more and more people began to share their similar feelings. Everyone on the planet does not share the same opinions, thoughts, or experiences, but many others do. Consider where the world would be if nobody had spoken up about a romantic attraction to the same gender. Homosexuality has become widely accepted in many countries. Simply because something is not in our understanding does not invalidate it. It is not "crazy."

Scientists are constantly uncovering new information about the human experience and the world around us. As we become more vocal, releasing the fear of judgment, they have more directions to research and study. You are not alone in your thoughts, experiences, and feelings. Tell your family, friends, and therapist. Other people will feel accepted to share theirs, too. Then we can be free to announce proudly, "I am not f*cking crazy!"

I almost died. I had what scientists refer to as a near death experience. My initial experience seems minor considering the stories I have read about, but nonetheless, it was an eye opener. The part I hesitated to talk about most was the meditation on my last day in the hospital that profoundly changed my life.

I began to realize my own fear of judgment as I shared my story, or rather *pieces* of the story, with different people in my circle. I often tell myself I don't care what others think when clearly, I do. Most religions and spiritual philosophies practice nonjudgment, but even the strongest believers still struggle to practice it. We are all human.

The bits I shared with my husband, mom, close family, spiritual bestie, yoga instructor-school classmates, my guru, and my acupuncturist all varied depending on my concerns or expectations of their reactions or judgments. We must trust in our loved ones and welcome their reactions with love in our heart—all of them.

Revisiting the Hospital Meditation

If you have seen some of the *X-Men* movie series, it will be easier to visualize what I saw during that meditation. If not, I know you will still get whatever message your spirit team is sending you by reading this book.

As I lay in my hospital bed, finally taking the nurse's advice and quieting my mind to meditate, I was suddenly in another place. I have felt the protection of angels surrounding me at various times in my life, and this was another one of those moments. I could feel love, protection, and peacefulness. This new place was in a completely dark space. Not dark in a scary way, just dark as in emptiness. Like being in space, only without stars. The image is kind of like the X-Men's Professor X wheeling out of the elevator into an abyss. Even now, years later, I can recall the image vividly.

I became aware I was standing in an empty space on what I can only describe as a spindle. I was in the center. I sensed I was standing, although it felt more like floating, in the center on a platform of some kind. Spinning around me as if I was the needle on a record player were beings. I couldn't tell how many angels, guides, protectors, and loved ones were surrounding me, but I felt completely safe and loved. It might have been my entire spirit team at first. I looked around, maybe spinning a bit myself. In awe for a moment. I tried to distinguish any image I could, which seemed to slow the spinning down.

I continued to concentrate on slowing the spinning enough to attempt to make out what and who were surrounding me. As the spinning slowed, some energetic beings faded into the background, and I observed four distinct platforms at the end of separate poles or spokes, all connected to my platform. The *X-Men* movie is the only visual comparison I can think of. We were in space—a blank darkness. I was in the middle. There were chrome spokes leading from my center platform out some distance, maybe the length of half a football field, to other platforms. They were equal distance apart and equal distance from me. It was a cross or plus sign with me in the center.

The platforms spun around me more and more slowly until I could recognize a figure or "being" on each one. At first, they were shadow-like, with a soft, semitransparent blue-white veil surrounding them. I recall asking, "Who are you?" as I would twist my body around to see the spinning platforms. The spinning eventually stopped with smoothness and grace. I saw Chin and Bellulah first. They were standing on opposite sides, almost directly in front and back of me. I looked to the right and still only saw the veiled being. I turned slightly to face the figure to my left as the Black man in the tan draped fabric came into focus. Again, in comparison to television, it was almost like when a character would teleport in *Star Trek*. It was less like molecules joining and more like pixels coming together in focus. I heard them all say in unison, "Slow down." It was softer and gentler this time. Spoken very slowly and distinctly. I was somehow able to spin myself around very slowly to look at each one of them, noting a loving expression on Bellulah's face and a simple expression of stillness on Chin.

I looked again at the being surrounded in the bluish-white veil and mentally asked it specifically, "Who are you?" I heard nothing but sensed an immense peace and calm. I tried to get an image of a person for a few moments and then heard a voice behind me, "You don't need to know." I turned around before coming to gaze at the newest member of my visually recognizable team of spirit guides. There was the man wrapped in a tan burlap type material like a toga, with a smirk on his face. I had not noticed a facial expression before. His smile was white, and his eyes were dark and kind. Fitting for his personality, he had a smirk rather than a supportive smile like Bellulah's.

"Why not?" I asked him. There was no verbal answer to hear, but there was a definite expression on his face as the answer. That expression of contempt, with the smirk gone and the eyes slightly narrowed, as if to ask "Seriously? Are you questioning me?" In defiance of the expression, I asked again. He answered this time, as he often does, with a question, "Why do you need to know?" I was stumped into silence for some time. I said, "OK, I *want* to know." An argument filled with both love and sarcasm began. He repeated his reply simply, "Why?" I honestly could not come up with an answer.

Instead, I shifted gears, drawing my attention to him directly. "OK, good point." I paused, then asked, "What's your name?" He answered, "It doesn't matter." His tone was matter of fact but gentle and softer than usual. "Yes, it does." I answered. Again, he asked "Why?" This time though, I had an answer.

"Because I need to call you something."

"Why?"

"So I have something to refer to you by."

"Why do you need to refer to me?"

My frustration began to fester. "Ugh. So I know what to call you."

Sensing my frustration, he said, "OK, call me whatever you want. My name doesn't matter."

"Fine. I will just call you a random name. Bob."

"If that makes you happy."

He knew I was satisfied, although a bit disgusted that we had to have such a ridiculous argument. Bellulah and Chin never gave me any trouble like this. With finality, I said, "Fine. Bob it is."

Before long, my curiosity led to more questions.

"How do you do that?" I asked.

"What?" Bob continued with his short responses which almost always cause me to pause and consider circumstances and aspects of a situation.

"Ask these questions I don't have answers to." I now realized "Bob" had always been the being I get rhetorical questions from on a regular basis. I've had the "Why do you care?" and "Why do you need to know?" questions many, many times. These questions usually do not have a real answer. It's usually a situation of "I want to know." Writing this now, I am getting the message that anything with the word "want" in my answer should be a true indicator that the question is stemming from the egoic mind. The ego always *wants* something.

He replied, "It is my way."

"What way?" I asked

"I know before you do, but I'm here to guide you, not answer everything for you. You are here for the lessons on this life journey." His lengthy response stunned me. I was grateful for the clarity and frustrated by the result.

I was acutely aware of the presence of the other three beings on the ends of each of their spokes. It felt as though I had a support team around me, like I could conquer anything. I pressed on, with my undeniably sarcastic tone, "What are you supposed to be? Like a Jedi or something?"

"If that is what you want to call it, sure."

As I was searching for an antagonistic response, I felt a surge of calmness surround me that came from the other three beings on the platforms. My frustration immediately shifted to a peaceful victorious contentment.

"Great. Then I will just call you Jedi Bob," I said, as a compromise.

"If that makes you feel better."

"Yes. Actually, it does," I concluded. "So, I guess you are just Jedi Bob from now on."

He just nodded with a slight smile of satisfaction and kindness. I looked around at the others, unable to recognize their visual images any longer. The spindle began to rotate again. I'm not sure if they were rotating around me or if I was spinning in the middle between them. Either way, it was a huge protective circle with me in the middle. I heard multiple voices at the same time. With finality in the tone, they very calmly said once again, "Just slow down."

They faded away. I was left floating in a blank space. Somehow, I knew that was it. They gave me the answer I had been searching for. The biggest, "Why?" I have ever asked, knowing it was for an important life lesson. The bonus was that I got so many answers and lessons during this meditation in the hospital that it was almost overwhelming.

I slowly opened my eyes. I wiped my eyes, blew my nose, and lay there in a bit of shock at what had just happened. It was undeniable. I didn't dream it. I looked at the clock and couldn't figure out if I misread the time before I closed my eyes. Only mere minutes had passed, but the whole ordeal seemed like it was hours. I guess it's true: there is no time on the other side.

There I was, left to contemplate what most would say was an unbelievable experience. Who would believe me? Would everyone call it crazy? Yet, I knew with all my heart it was real—definitely unexpected and different, but real.

I received so many answers. The "reasons" (or rather, lessons, if I allowed them to be) could be summed up and shared with others.

The spirit team had to bring me to the very brink of death for me to open my eyes and ears to receive messages and guidance. If I ignore signs and shut them out, they (angels, guides, loved ones) will go to any lengths to get my attention. They will hit me over the head with a two-by-four in the hardest, most drastic, unignorable way possible. We must not ignore our spirit team or shut them out.

We don't need answers to all our questions. Sometimes no answer and inconclusiveness are OK. Accept things or experience things to be in the present moment. There is no need to jump to a final point. There may not even be one! Listen and consider all sides or aspects of what you want to know. Embrace the journey. Search for *guidance*, not answers.

We all have many, many beings on our spirit team. It is not imperative to have a name or visual image to identify a specific angel or guide. It is not important to know which loved one's presence is sensed. Sometimes an energy is identifiable by attitude or tone. Sometimes having their love, guidance, and protection is all that matters. And sometimes, the identification will be discovered or known. I recognize some angels by their energies, and I can now identify three of my spirit guides. Most times, I know who is with me from the other side. It is convenient to have identifications, albeit unnecessary. However, I will continue to attempt to identify recognizable traits to assist in describing and discussing members of my spirit team.

Finally, the big message: Slow down. Self-care is the highest priority.

There is nothing more important than your health. Because without it, without *you*, all the things you make top priorities: stretching yourself too thin, pushing yourself too hard, and helping others before helping yourself are absolutely not going to be possible if you don't remain healthy enough to do any of it. Slow down to care for yourself. Slow down to observe life. Slow down to appreciate life's gifts. Slow down to listen and feel. Meditate! Just. Slow. Down.

As I have released the fear of judgment and learned to raise my vibration to connect to the frequency of positive universal love energy, I have been guided to write this book. I stood at death's door and saw angels. I came back from the very brink of it all ending. I thought that was the two-by-four. I meditated and talked with my spirit guides.

Perhaps it was that life-changing meditation that was the two-by-four. Regardless, I know I am not crazy and that sharing the experience with others is the best way for everyone to realize their abilities and gifts without believing they are crazy.

Kendra Bergman

Mindfulness Exercise | *Slow Down*

In a quiet space, free of distractions, settle yourself into a comfortable position. Notice your breathing. Is it fast? Slow? Uneven? Think back to previous exercises that asked you to even out your breathing by pacing it rhythmically. As your breath slows, observe your thoughts. You can slow down any racing thoughts simply by allowing them to rise and fall, without latching onto them. The key to this exercise is coming back to it with some frequency: nightly, before work, a few times a week, whatever works best for you. Afterward, use the space provided to write down how you plan to take time to slow down in your life.

And What about Free Will?

Nothing can prevent your picture from coming into concrete form except the same power which gave you birth—yourself.
—Genevieve Behrend

Through free will, we have the choice to block or ignore the voices and messages, but to ignore and block out the messages does not serve us well. When your life path remains out of alignment for too long, the Universe will shake you to awaken you. You may experience the proverbial two-by-four; it could be a mental break, a serious illness, the loss of a loved one. It might not be as drastic, but only if you are paying attention and listening. When we ignore messages from our spirit team, we put up blocks that alter the frequency; like changing a radio station dial.

Release the urge to question everything you are hearing. Release the impulse to dismiss yourself as crazy.

Sometimes I find my egoic mind wondering about other people. *How does she do that? What does he think of that?* Then I will hear the spirit team, "It doesn't matter. It's none of your business. Why do you care?" It's not always a recognizable being. The real gift is knowing it is someone on my spirit team. It could be one or more angels, guides, or loved ones from the other side. That doesn't matter either. That is what Jedi Bob's whole point was during the hospital meditation.

I am a determined person. I am also the type of person who constantly seeks answers or "proof" of something. I want to know how and why something is the way it is. I have even questioned how it came to be known that two plus two equals four. Who started counting anyway? There is that little voice in my head again. *Why does it matter?* It boils down to faith. There are things we accept in life as fact. Two plus two equals four. There are twenty-four hours in a day. The earth rotates around the sun. There are other planets. Now I've even heard there are other universes, making this one a multiverse. Skeptical, yes. But humans are also believers. We have come to trust science and the media. We see a video or image, knowing it can be altered, and still believe something is true. Why? Because we have faith. We have hope. When I hear, feel, see, or get a knowingness of something others would question, I have faith in myself. I trust myself, and I trust my spirit team.

Lessons Learned

There was a long road to recovery ahead of me once I was discharged from the hospital; this was not only a physical challenge, but an emotional and mental challenge as well. I felt like my spiritual health was finally on track and kept me motivated in the months that passed. I continued to listen to my spirit team with an open mind, though it wasn't easy. Even now, balancing between listening and being overwhelmed with messages is still a practice for me, and discernment of the messages is a gift that is still in the process of growing and developing. It probably always will be.

One of the messages I kept getting was, "Call Serena." I met her at a yoga retreat six months prior. In addition to the group classes she attended, Serena offered individual "chi boosts" with a brief session of acupuncture combined with sound healing. I had never experienced sound healing before that retreat and was intrigued. Even though there was no doubt that acupuncture would benefit me, as with the other messages, I chose to ignore the persistent nudge to schedule a regular session. But fearful of what would happen to my physical health if I did not follow the guidance, I decided it was time I contacted her.

I reached out to Serena via email to schedule a consultation. Within a few weeks I was in her office, and after a thorough questionnaire and exam, I was in treatment with her every two weeks.

The benefits and improvements were immediate! Although Serena worked on my energetic and physical health, the sessions with her had a huge impact on my emotional, mental, and spiritual health as well. Finally, I had hope for a full recovery. One session with Serena was like six sessions in one. I received a Chinese medicine exam, acupuncture, acupressure massage, nutritional and energy counseling, sound healing, and (what I considered) a version of a therapy session too!

I clearly needed someone to talk to about the emotional turmoil I was in. Because I have always been someone who takes action, it was difficult for me not to feel like I was being lazy when my lack of energy made it hard for me to maintain the stamina to do anything. Even simple tasks like walking from the car into a store would wear me out. The best advice Serena gave me that year was, "Rest is not doing nothing. Rest is an action." When our physical body needs to recover, it needs rest to do so.

Where Am I Now?

That figurative smack over the head with the two-by-four has reminded me many times to keep my eyes and ears open. Even with a consistent spiritual practice, I still get busy and preoccupied with tasks and responsibilities, sometimes tuning out my spirit team in one way or another. However, I take a moment every morning and every night to open myself up to any messages from the universe and my spirit team; I may dismiss some messages, but they can be relentless.

One of my teachers says, "A message will not clear until it is addressed," meaning if it is important, our spirit team will continue to give us the signs, symbols, and messages until we process what they are telling us. Even when we get off track—even if we are *way* off track—the Universe will guide us back to our path, the path to help the other souls we were brought into this life to impact.

I also have many teachers, mentors, and guides on my earthly spirit team as well as my "earth angels." The Universe brings us together for the greater good. Each of us is meant to help others along the way. I've often had the image of a relay race where one person hands the baton to another. One person is not better or the leader. They are simply passing the baton.

When we allow life to flow, we notice how we transition from one growth point or awakening moment to another. What I know now is to keep an open mind and a high vibration with a heart full of love. No task is more important than maintaining our spiritual health because without it, our emotional and mental health decline, leading to physical health problems that can cause us to spiral out of control. At that point, whatever tasks we thought were important become virtually impossible.

As challenging as they have been, I am incredibly grateful for all the two-by-four moments in my life. As my friend and mentor Julie Jancius says, "Sometimes Spirit has to shake you to awaken you." We are all experiencing a spiritual awakening. It is a continual process. Part of the process is releasing the fear of judgment to share our experiences, lessons, knowledge, and wisdom with others. To those we are here to help along the path of life, it will make sense. For those who do not yet understand or refuse to accept what we know is real, let them have their opinion that we are woo-woo, whackadoo, and crazy. I am simply here to tell you that what you see, hear, feel, and *know* is real.

Seriously. Have faith and believe in yourself and your spirit team. You are not f*cking crazy.

Resources and Recommended Reading

1. Sylvia Browne, *Life on the Other Side; Contacting Your Spirit Guide; The Other Side and Back*

2. Rhonda Byrne, *The Secret*

3. Deepak Chopra, *Meta Human: Unleashing Your Infinite Potential; Total Meditation*

4. Dr. Joe Dispenza, *Morning and Evening Meditation: Being Defined by a Vision of the Future Instead of a Memory from the Past*

5. Dr. Wayne Dyer, *Memories of Heaven*

6. Louise Hay, *Meditations to Heal Your Life*

7. Julie Jancius, *Angels and Awakening: A Guide to Raise Your Vibration and Hear Your Angels*

8. Jack Kornfield, *Guided Meditations for Self-Healing; After the Ecstasy, the Laundry: How the Heart Grows Wise on the Spiritual Path*

9. Goswami Kriyananda, *The Spiritual Science of Kriya Yoga; Pathway to God- Consciousness; Beginner's Guide to Meditation*

10. Joel Olsteen, *I Declare; Rule Your Day*

11. Don Miguel Ruiz, *The Four Agreements*

12. Eckhart Tolle, *The Power of Now; Stillness Speaks; The Importance of Being Extraordinary*

Works Cited

1. Cleveland Clinic. Brain Facts. "Healthy Brains." April 12, 2021. https://healthybrains.org/brain-facts/

2. Tolle, Eckhart. *A New Earth*. October 6, 2005.

About the Author

Kendra Bergman is forever a student of spirituality. Her interest in spiritual growth began when she met her first mentor while working at a local day spa in 1994. She is a certified Angel Reiki Master, Chakra Healer, LifeForce Energy Healer, and Yoga Instructor. Kendra is passionate about helping all humankind understand and connect with their Higher Self, encouraging the awakening of their intuition and the creative powers that lie within them. She lives in the American Southwest and enjoys family time and gardening.

Printed in the United States
by Baker & Taylor Publisher Services